Addictions: What All Parents Need to Know to Survive the Drug Epidemic

by Rev. Dr. Kevin T. Coughlin Ph.D.

KTC Publishing Phase IIC Coaching, LLC

This book is a work of nonfiction.

First Printing

Copyright © 2016 Rev. Dr. Kevin T. Coughlin Ph.D.

KTC Publishing Phase IIC Coaching, LLC

All Rights Reserved.

As permitted under the US Copyright Act of 1976, no part of this publication may be reproduced, distributed, or transmitted in any form or by any means (electronic, mechanical, photocopying, recording, or otherwise, stored in a database or retrieval system, without prior written permission of the copyright holder of this book, except by a reviewer, who may quote brief passages in a review.

The scanning, uploading, and distribution of this book via the Internet or other means without the written permission of the copyright holder and publisher is illegal and punishable by law. Please purchase only authorized electronic editions, and do not participate in or encourage electronic piracy of copyrighted materials. Your support of the author is appreciated.

Printed in the United States of America

ISBN 978-0-9977006-9-5 (paperback)

Foreword

By Author, Arnie Wexler, CCGC & Sheila Wexler, LCADC, CCGC

Rev. Dr. Kevin T. Coughlin's book: Addictions: What Every Parent Needs to Know to Survive the Drug Epidemic is a must have guide for anyone who is trying to understand how to cope with a loved one caught in the web of the disease of addiction. This best-selling author's work with regard to addiction education, prevention, and awareness has already helped to change and save thousands of lives. This book gives real life examples that empower families with all of the knowledge and information needed to find hope and help. It's rare to find someone with the expert knowledge and experience of this author. This book will help change and save many lives, you can bet on it!

I think it's important to talk about drug addiction, teens, and explain what it feels like and what it looks like, and then talk about the family and the family member who's addicted. Sheila has seen firsthand how drug addiction has ravaged the addicts and their families, as Sheila has run a drug treatment facility for many years, along with treatment from addicted and problem gambling. This book is exceptional, and vital for all parents and grandparents to read.

I was about twelve years old when I broke a lady's window, and she hollered out, "If your father were alive you wouldn't be behaving like this!" Up till that time, I had no idea that my father was not alive, he died when I was two years old. I couldn't get passed that thought at the time.

I am a compulsive gambler; the first time I went to the racetrack I was fourteen years old was making fifty cents an hour working after school. One night I won fifty-four dollars at the racetrack. That win changed my life; all of a sudden first time in my life, I felt equal or better than anybody else. (It was the big win!)

I was hooked! By age seventeen, I was stealing to support my gambling addiction; it took until age thirty for me to get into recovery. My last bet was April 10, 1968.

I want to share with you now about a family I know very well. Their daughter had to be put in a treatment center for drugs and drinking at age fifteen, she came out of treatment and was clean five years. At age twenty, she went back to her addiction and developed other addictions: gambling and food. Her family kept enabling and bailing her out for over twenty years of her manipulating the family.

The family thought that enabling and bailed her out would help her get into recovery again; it was never-ending they were doing anything and everything to try to help her. Their daughter eventually became pregnant and had a baby boy and still continued her addiction and the family still continued their addiction of enabling and bailing her out. Now they saw it as helping their grandson. When the grandson was twelve the grandparents took the grandson to live with them as their daughter was still into addictions (to save the grandsons life). The grandson's history was his dad was an active addict and he had only seen his dad three times in his life, and his mother was into her addiction.

At fifteen, he started to smoke pot it got worse at seventeen; he was born with the addiction gene. The grandparents helped get him into treatment, he was clean a year and relapsed, they got him into treatment again; however, he ran away after two weeks. The grandparents changed their locks and the code to get into their home. Their grandson in not in recovery today but the grandparents are not making the same mistake they did with their daughter so many years ago. No enabling or bailouts! After putting their life on hold for six years to try to save their grandson the grandparents are back to living their life today...

Arnie and Sheila Wexler have provided extensive training on Compulsive, Problem, and Underage Gambling, to more than 40,000 gaming employees (personnel and executives) and have written Responsible Gaming Programs for major gaming companies. In addition, they have worked with Gaming Boards and Regulators, presented educational workshops nationally and internationally and have provided expert witness testimony. Sheila Wexler is the Executive Director of the Compulsive Gambling Foundation. They also run a national help line (888 LAST BET) www.aswexler.com Arnie coauthored the amazing book: All Bets Are Off: Losers, Liars, and Recovery from Gambling Addiction in 2015 with Steve Jacobson.

"Arnie placed his last bet 4/10/68"

Arnie Wexler CCGC
Sheila Wexler CCGC, LCADC

Addictions: What All Parents Need to Know to Survive the Drug Epidemic has been used successfully by numerous individuals, residential recovery programs, out-patient programs, professional recovery coaches, aftercare professionals, counselors, therapists, probation officers, ministries, recovery retreats, sponsors, sober companions, and family members to help them to get a deeper understanding of the disease of addiction, the solution to the problem, and the program of action that promotes change in the substance abuser. A Support system for family and friends of substance abusers that helps to provide clarity, understanding, education, prevention, and awareness.

PLEASE VISIT www.theaddiction.expert for other books written and published by Rev. Dr. Kevin T. Coughlin Ph.D., there you can join his mailing list for advanced notice on his next book.

Disclaimer: In this book, the author shares his experience, strength, and hope with readers, this should not be considered advice. All information in this book is for informational and educational purposes, not medical or psychiatric advice or to prescribe the use of any technique as a form of treatment for medical or psychiatric problems without the advice of a physician, psychiatrist or appropriate licensed professional either directly or indirectly. In the event you use any of the information in this book for yourself, neither the author, nor the publisher accepts responsibility for your actions.

Table of Contents

Foreword 3
Introduction 1
Chapter One Parents Need Facts on Addiction 3
Chapter Two It Takes a Village 10
Chapter Two A Emerging Street Drugs 24
Chapter Three The Disease Model of Addiction & The Twelve-Step Modality of Recovery 31
Chapter Four Meet the Professional Recovery Coach 38
Chapter Five Codependency, Enabling and the Family 42
Chapter Six Helping Parents of Substance Abusers Deal with Misdirected Anger 49
Chapter Seven Dual Diagnosis 53
Chapter Eight Twelve Tips to Stay Sober Through the Holidays 57
Chapter Nine AMA/ APA: Leaving Against Medical or Professional Advice 62
Chapter Ten Grandparents: The Unsung Heroes of Addiction Epidemic 72
Chapter Eleven Signs of Drug Use & Keys to Family Recovery 75
Chapter Twelve Suicides & Overdoses are Reality 80
Chapter Thirteen The Importance of Commitment 90
Chapter Fourteen Parents Use Your Words Wisely 92
Chapter Fifteen Important Terms & Definitions 97
Chapter Sixteen My Heroes 110
About The Author 5
Rev. Dr. Kev.'s Publication Credits 3

Introduction

When I was seven years old, I accompanied my mother to many twelve-step recovery meetings and witnessed the miracle as it changed her life and mine. A few decades later, the twelve-steps saved my life, my brother's life, his wife's life, my uncle's life, and countless friend's lives. After witnessing the power of the twelve-step process my family, friends, and I opened a twelve-step recovery program and retreat in The Poconos of Pennsylvania for adult men and women who suffer from addiction. Over the past two decades, the thousands of miracles that I have witnessed, and lives saved are due to the twelve-step process. We found that this process was a spiritual program of action, based on spiritual principles.

I felt it was my obligation to share what I have learned over the past forty-seven years about addiction, the solution to addiction, and the program of action that leads to long-term sobriety. The disease of addiction impacts the whole family and the community. I've witnessed the wreckage and the death from addiction. My goal is to educate, make families aware, and have prevention become a priority. I originally became clean and sober at a twelve-step retreat that was started by one of the Founders of Alcoholics Anonymous, Bill W., it was at this retreat that I started to realize that I had a calling on my life to help other sick and suffering alcoholics and substance abusers.

After two decades of teaching on addiction recovery, spirituality, and the twelve-step process, and developing my skills as a professional writer, it only made sense to combine the two and share this life-saving information with a larger audience. My mom passed on five years ago with over forty years of sobriety, and today I celebrate nineteen years!

My dream is to share my knowledge with as many individuals as I can during my lifetime, building an army of spiritual addiction recovery professionals who can help save lives. It doesn't matter if you are reading this book for yourself, a family member, or a dear friend; the information contained within the pages here can be life changing. I know that recovery from addiction changed and saved my life!

They say in the rooms of recovery, if you want what we have, and are willing to go to any length to get it, you will recover. All you have to do is want it, and do the footwork. This amazing book will aid you on your journey as you walk in the sunlight of the spirit. My personal website is www.revkevsrecoveryworld.com I hope you will visit. Best of life!

Chapter One
Parents Need Facts on Addiction

Parents raise their children for almost two decades. The fortunate ones don't experience drug addiction or alcoholism. For those not so fortunate, they enter a dark place that will change their world forever. The child that they have raised for sixteen to twenty years of age becomes a total stranger in their home. The parents are living with a junkie, an alcoholic, and a drug dealer and they don't even know it. The truth is addiction can strike at any age; no one is exempt. The big question is how do parents know if their kids are on drugs?

Don't wait until it's too late; parents aren't supposed to bury their children.

Too many parents wait until it's too late to find out the answer to this hard question. This is a very complex situation that is being complicated by economic pressures, homelessness, joblessness, and lack of affordability of education. The breakdown of the family unit, lack of supervision, children are starving for structure and guidance. Broken homes, lack of male role models in the home especially for boys, and lack of a female role model for girls is a big part of the problem.

Some parents don't want to know the truth because it's too painful to face. Some parents already know the truth, but they're in denial. Some families are so dysfunctional that the parents don't even care! Some parents are addicts themselves. Some parents are such horrible enablers that they can't see the forest through the trees.

The ends to addiction are jails, institutions, and death, so it's important that we educate parents. Parents are not supposed to bury their children.

Our children are dying; the time to do something is now!

I've answered the phone calls at 3:00 AM and listened to the blood-curdling screams of mothers telling me that their sons or daughters had overdosed and died minutes ago. There is nothing to be said, no words that can comfort, it's too late! I've stood in the cemeteries and watched the fathers cry as their sons and daughters were buried. It's almost unbearable to watch. The time to do something is now!

I also want to mention that Pathological Gambling is three to four times more likely to affect teenagers than older people. Problem Gambling is the number one addiction related to suicide. One in five Pathological Gamblers will attempt suicide.

Opiate addiction was epidemic in 2014 and still is in 2016. Marijuana is still frequently used by young people. Cocaine has dropped in popularity with young people probably because of cost. Prescription drugs are still prevalent. Some of the most popular are Ambien, Dilaudid, Xanax, Adderall, Oxycontin, Opana, etc. There are also over the counter drugs that are very dangerous; Dextromethorphan is one of the worst. The kids call it Robo-Tripping. Then there are new "legal" drugs that pop up like Bath Salts, Salvia, Hawaiian Gold, etc. some of these are already illegal, but may not be detectable in a drug screening. Let's not forget alcohol, plenty of damage can be caused by alcohol alone. New emerging trends: Caffeine Powder, one teaspoon equivalent to twenty-five cups of coffee, "Krokodil" a toxic homemade opioid used as a heroin substitute, causes flesh destroying, gangrenous at injection sites, "N-Bomb", being sold as" legal acid", "Smiles", or "251" generally found in liquid or powder form, or soaked into blotter paper, responsible for many deaths, "Syrup", "Purple Drank", "Sizzurp", "Lean" contains codeine cough syrup and promethazine, has caused many fatal overdoses, "Molly", MDMA in pill form known as "Ecstasy" many dangerous chemicals are mixed in them, consequences include death, "Gravel", looks like salt, comes in many colors, a mix of Klonopin, Meth, and "Bath salts." A very dangerous drug! Now there is "Flakka" a brutal drug!"

It is an amphetamine, just like Molly. This synthetic stimulant contains alpha –PVP which was banned and labeled a schedule 1 drug by the US DEA in 2014 the drug has flooded the South Florida, Texas, and Ohio areas. It initially increases dopamine, the brain's pleasure chemical, you become alert and euphoric. The side effects are aggression, irregular heartbeat, seizures, hallucinations, delusions, and death.

D.A.W.N., The Drug Abuse Warning Network data show that Emergency Department visits involving the nonmedical use of gabapentin have increased by approximately ninety percent in the United States since 2008.

"With enough information, it is almost impossible "not" to predict people's action." – Idries Shah

Education, Awareness, and Prevention is the only way that professionals and families can stay on top in the war on addiction. Many of the medications that we all thought would be helpful in the fight against addiction are becoming addictive substances that are problematic, not problem solvers. Medications such as Suboxone and Subutex are now a big problem, where they were originally thought to be the miracle drug to solve addiction. You can add Gabapentin to the list of problem medications.

Take an honest look at any changes. There are so many drugs, so many new drugs, legal drugs, legal drugs that become illegal drugs, over the counter dangerous drugs, and alcohol. Don't focus on that but focus on the following: Look for signs and symptoms, behavioral issues, changes in personal appearance, changes in habit, changes auto and home, and health issues.

If you have reason to believe that someone you love has a problem with drugs or alcohol, the first thing to do is ask them. Do you have a problem with drugs or alcohol? Are you in trouble? They may not tell you the truth; denial is part of the problem. It is worth the try.

Take an honest look at any changes in behavioral issues. Is your teen buying poker books, playing poker for money online, or betting on sports? Is there a change in relationships at home and friends? Is there a loss of inhibitions? Have there been drastic mood swings and changes? Have there been signs of being withdrawn or depression? Did they stop communicating or go silent? Are they full of excuses? Are they acting out, being hostile? Are they lethargic, abnormal sleep patterns, can't focus?

How about personal appearance? Is their appearance suddenly messy, careless? Is their hygiene poor? Do they have track marks on their arms or legs? Do they have pinned pupils? Do they have a flushed red face?

Look at their personal habit changes. Do their clothes suddenly smell like smoke? Do they avoid eye contact? Are they going out every night? Do they sometimes have large bankrolls? Do they have cash flow problems? Do they have secretive phone calls? Do they suddenly get the munchies? Have they started using air fresheners, incense, colognes?

How about home and auto changes? Are there unusual smells in the car? Have prescriptions disappeared from the house? Have valuables or money gone missing? Is there any missing alcohol? Any rolled up dollar bills or cut straws? Is there any aluminum foil with black or gray abstract lines? Unusual seeds, wrappers, or containers? Are there any bottles, pipes, bongs, foil, lighters in the car? Any powder residue on any surfaces?

Take a look at health issues: is your loved one frequently sick? Do they often have a runny nose? Do they often have cotton mouth? Has there been any drastic weight gain or loss? Has there been any depression? Do they often have headaches? Are they frequently nauseous and sick in the early part of the day?

How are things going at school and work? Have they lost interest? Are their grades tanking? Do they have any interest in extracurricular activities? Do they fulfill their responsibilities?

I wonder if I asked most parents, "When is the last time you had a sit down real heart to heart conversation with your kid?" What would they say? It's so important to communicate, and listening is the most powerful form of communication that we have.

Are there drugs hidden in your house? What would you say to the police if they came to your house with a search warrant, telling you that drugs have been sold out of your house for the past six months? Some good places to look, but remember drugs could be hidden anywhere, in holes in mattresses, under loose planks in the floor, CD/DVD cases in the ceiling, toilet tank, coffee cans, cereal boxes. There are a million places to hide drugs, as far as the imagination reaches. State and Federal law enforcement have been seizing people's homes and property because their kids have sold drugs from the home. It turns into a living nightmare for the parents, as they battle to get their homes back.

Welcome to the epidemic, the war.

If you're very fortunate, you have a normal teenager! If not, welcome to the war! Talk with your partner or spouse about suspected drug use, you must work together. Be prepared to be called a hypocrite by the addict in the family. Collect as much evidence of drug and or alcohol use as you can before confrontation. Expect denial and anger from the family addict, that's normal. Plan for an expected outcome, you must be prepared before you execute. Spell out house rules and consequences for drug use. Recognize the significance of addiction in the family. Remind the family addict of the family support. Know that you are not alone. There are wonderful support groups for the family. Families Anonymous, Al-Anon are two such groups.

If you determine that your son or daughter has a problem with drug addiction or alcoholism, there is a plethora of help available to you. The problem that you are going to come across is all the miss-information and bad advice on addiction and recovery.

How do you know what is best for your son or daughter? Families need to understand the problem, only utilize programs that are tried, tested, and proven. Not theories. A support network, including a fellowship, seems to work best for this purpose. Addicts are sick people; don't expect them to act like normal people overnight. Recovery is a process; it takes time. If you walk twenty miles into the woods, then you will have to walk twenty miles to get out of the woods. It's important not to put conditions on love, and at the same time, to hold addicted loved ones accountable and responsible for their actions. There must be consequences for all actions. Accountability and responsibility demonstrate the willingness necessary to recover. Daily attitudes and choices will dictate the quality of each's future.

There is help to recover, and no son or daughter has to die from this disease.

Spirituality is simply saying yes to life! Recovery is all about breaking the chains of self-burden, and learning to live in freedom. Recovery is about learning to walk in the sunlight of the spirit one day at a time. Recovery is about learning to be a part of the world, instead of the world revolving around the individual. Recovery is about change and growth!

Whatever your problems are, there are others that have had the same problems and have worked through them for a better life. Many people die each year from addiction; most never make it into the rooms of recovery. Do whatever you need to do, to get between your loved ones and drugs. Their lives may depend on it. Active substance abusers are blind to reality; give them a reality check. Hold the mirror up to the addict's face, tell him how you feel. If you're an addicted person, get help now! As powerful as addiction is, love is more powerful!

You can love the substance abuser back to health; sometimes tough love is needed. Good choices should be rewarded; bad choices must come with consequences. Most active addicts feel helpless and hopeless.

Addicts need all the support that they can get: the support of the family, of addiction professionals such as recovery coaches, the support of the recovery fellowship, and a sponsor.

There is help to recover, and no substance abuser has to die from this disease. The ends to addiction are jails, institutions, and death, or recovery. If you have an addiction problem, please get some help. If someone you know has an addiction problem, help them to see the truth, and help them to get help. Addiction is spiritual bankruptcy. The more we educate, the more power we have to fight addiction. All those beautiful young souls did not die in vain; because of them, we are all more aware going forward to help families and our youth in the war against addiction. Together we all can save this life! Prevention, awareness, and education will save thousands of young lives.

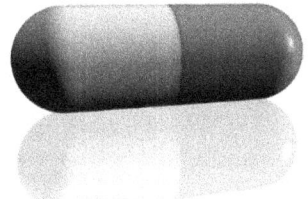

Chapter Two
It Takes a Village

There is a saying in the rooms of twelve-step recovery programs, "The definition of insanity is doing the same thing over and over and expecting different results!" Sometimes I wonder if they're talking about the pathology of addiction of describing the current paradigm of treatment. Short-term treatment is not effective. This is not an attempt to condemn or pass blame; it is an effort to find better solutions to an insidious disease. Our young are dying in record numbers there must be a more practical solution to the problem.

In today's recovery world, experience and science have shown us that the addicted person's family must also be addressed, not just the addicted person. Addiction has proven itself to be a family disease. Not necessarily that more than one person in the family is addicted, but the whole family is affected by the disease. The family needs to understand addiction and recovery so that they can support recovery without enabling addiction. They need to be educated as to the true pathology of addiction. The problem defines the solution. There are no short cuts; there is no easier way out. I heard someone say the other day, "It takes a village" to help the addict to recover.

Think about the facts. How do most people start off recovery? If they're willing to get help, they go to detox, if not they have an intervention, or take more lumps. Then they go to a short-term stay in a residential program. (Less than ninety days.) A professional drives the process. Then there is total disengagement. The family may not even communicate with anyone else but their addicted family member. Their loved one returns home, and the family thinks that their loved one is cured. Does this sound familiar and about right? This process doesn't work! Treatment works, the process does not.

Let's look at some of the problems. Not every person that needs help gets help. More than fifty percent of the people who go for treatment don't stay to complete the program, and their families enable them. Only a small minority get continuing care. Most people don't get a long enough stay for initial treatment. Most people relapse within a year of treatment, those that consume alcohol and other drugs relapse within ninety days. Those that have a high rate of recovery and low rate of relapse get there at between four and five years of remission. The professionals have all disengaged with the addicted person when they need more help.

Based on my training and observation, it is my opinion that the recovery world is about to undergo a major paradigm shift in addiction recovery treatment. There has to be more focus on post-treatment. There needs to be continuing education for the whole family of those suffering from addiction, professionals, peers, and those addicted. Everyone needs to have a coach! Recovery coaches for those addicted, family recovery coaches for the families. The whole process needs to be results and client driven. There need to be case managers externally from treatment programs that monitor from assessment to disengagement which should not conclude prior to five years. Early reintervention when needed. Just like everyone links up to social media, those addicted will need to link up with recovery communities. We also need to continue to develop recovery community resources, learning as we go. Give more credibility to those with years of addiction recovery, they know what works and what doesn't. Give reasonable choices to those addicted in different modalities.

Addiction treatment and recovery isn't as simple as just not using illicit drugs and alcohol. Recovery is about changing the way that the person thinks and lives. Recovery is a lifetime commitment. It's about saying yes to life and doing the next right thing. Recovery is a gift to the hopeless and dying. We all need to work together for a better future. Recovery is as much about the spirit as it is about the mind and body.

Science alone will never find the answer, nor will religion, or government policy makers. It will take the whole village!

Addiction treatment today

Can any problem be solved? Some people believe that every problem defines its own solution; if you completely understand the problem, then you can find a solution. Those who cannot find solutions have perspective and perception problems. In other words, they are blocked and need to change their worldview and vantage point. There are many ways to look at both problems and solutions.

Today I 'Googled' the words "Addiction Treatment" and there were 28,900,000 entries. I entered the question: "What is an addiction?" and got 48,000000 results. According to The National Institute on Drug Abuse, substance abuse costs our nation over $600 billion annually. Treatment is less expensive than other alternatives such as incarceration, treatment provides healthcare savings, and lowers social costs.

Conservative estimates say that for every buck invested in addiction recovery programs, they reduce criminal-justice costs by between four and seven dollars; reducing drug-related crime; and theft. Savings related to health care can increase to a ratio of twelve to one. Savings come from fewer relationship conflicts, drug-related accidents, and overdoses, and greater productivity in the workplace.

Let's take a look at some of the models of addiction treatment available today:

1. Abstinence: zero tolerance
2. Harm Reduction/ Moderation Management: Some but not drug of choice
3. Twelve-Step: Abstinence with meetings and step-work, Sponsor, Higher-Power
4. Faith-Based: Specific to certain religions

5. Medication Management: Suboxone, Subutex, "Bupe", Methadone, Vivitrol
6. Holistic: Fitness, Yoga, wellness, health, exercise, alternative therapies, and meditation
7. Smart Recovery: Self-empowerment, self-reliance, no higher-power, will-power, meetings

Models of Addiction and Addiction Treatment that are used today include:

1. The Minnesota Model: thirty-day Residential, twelve-step, Relapse Prevention, Denial, Drug-screening, AA/NA.
2. Disease Process vs. Disorder: Sick vs. Empowered
3. Non-twelve-Step Models: Smart Recovery, Holistic.
4. The Florida Model: Halfway and Sober Houses for Aftercare
5. The twelve-Step Model: (Used in Florida and Minnesota Models)

There are several styles of addiction treatment starting with detox, where the substance abuser is placed to have chemicals removed from their system and may be given medication management. Residential treatment programs, which usually span twenty-eight to thirty days and cost between $8,000 and $75,000. Partial Hospitalization programs (PHPs) which are day treatments lasting about thirty days, and cost between $10,000 and $35,000. Intensive outpatient programs (IOPs), which are typically six weeks in length, encompass meeting three times per week and cost between $8,000 and $35,000. Halfway houses and sober houses are usually six-month stays with zero tolerance for relapse, curfews, or failed drug tests. Clients must hold jobs earning them between $150 to $750 a week. Twelve-step meetings are free.

"We are our choices." – Jean-Paul Sartre

I would like to examine each model individually based on facts and statistics.

First, let's look at medication management. Is it necessary to replace one powerful drug with another powerful drug?

It seems these medications may serve a purpose short-term for detoxification over a four- to-six-week period. However, many doctors want to keep clients on these medications long-term. Any physician in America, who takes an eight-hour, online course about Suboxone can obtain authorization to prescribe it. Most of these doctors know very little about addiction; it's far out of the scope of their training. Most Suboxone doctors don't know how to get clients off of the Suboxone. There have been no studies from the medical community on long-term effects of being on Suboxone or how to get a patient off of it. Buprenorphine can produce euphoria, cause dependency, and cause a high. Statistics say that ninety-five percent of individuals trying to get off of Suboxone fail. Methadone is extremely difficult to get off of and has been attributed to numerous deaths.

Is Suboxone a "miracle drug," or just a "cash cow" for Big Pharma? A recent investigation by The New York Times began to expose the hard-hitting tactics used by manufacturers to find physicians who were interested in making barrels full of cash by converting opiate addicts into Suboxone users for life. The Times article alleges that Suboxone's manufacturer attempted to manipulate the FDA approval process in order to monopolize the painkiller-substance abuser market. It was quite easy for the manufacturers to convince doctors that opiate addicts needed to be on Suboxone for maintenance because of the belief that painkiller addicts cannot ever be free from addiction. The thinking is, that opiate addicts have permanently damaged their neurology from the use of drugs.

"I didn't know you could overdose on Suboxone." – **Mr.** **Verrill** said in an interview at a federal prison in Otisville, New York.

Suboxone's revenue is estimated at more than $150 billion dollars in the United States last year. Funds generated from sales aided federal officials to finance development, and promotion Suboxone as safer than methadone.

Buprenorphine (also known as "Bupe") is considered both legal and illicit. Legal when prescribed by doctors and illegal when sold on the street, by dealers and in prisons.

In 2002, buprenorphine was approved by the FDA as a treatment for opiate dependence. Buprenorphine has been associated with deaths due to breathing problems, especially when used in combination with other drugs and alcohol.

Subutex (buprenorphine hydrochloride) and Suboxone (buprenorphine hydrochloride and naloxone hydrochloride) were created to help stop opiate addiction by preventing symptoms of withdrawal from opiates. Subutex contains buprenorphine only and is designed to use at the beginning of treatment for opiate addiction.

Suboxone, contains buprenorphine and an antagonist naloxone, Suboxone is designed to be used as maintenance treatment for opiate dependence. Naloxone has been added to Suboxone to protect against intravenous abuse of buprenorphine by individuals physically dependent on opiates. Subutex and Suboxone come in 2 mg and 8 mg tablets which are dissolved under the tongue. Patients become physically dependent on Suboxone and Subutex, which are manufactured by the British company, Reckitt Benckiser Pharmaceuticals. (The company who manufactures Lysol.)

Buprenorphine can produce euphoria, dependency, and cause a buzz. There is a large "black market" for substance abusers who buy their own drugs. Prison officials say that the Suboxone is nicknamed "prison heroin" and the new dissolvable filmstrip is a popular form of contraband.

According to The New York Times's analysis of federal data, Suboxone was a "primary suspect" in 420 deaths in our nation since 2003; however, it seems that no one wants to know about the potential problem. It seems that there is an escalating problem.

A prosecuting attorney from Michigan was quoted as saying "Arrest after arrest of people who are possessing or abusing Suboxone, who don't have a prescription for it, who are shooting it up and who are snorting it." Portland officials say that there is an unstoppable amount of Suboxone on the street where addicts are injecting it.

In 2009, the RDA approved a generic Subutex, buprenorphine without the abuse deterrent, even though Reckitt Benckiser tried to stop it. The cost was one-third of Suboxone. After 2009, Reckitt Benckiser built its Suboxone sales force to approximately two hundred, paid between four and five hundred doctors as advocates, and paid $100,000 in dues to the American Society of Addiction Medicine, as they lobbied for influence, according to former employees. (In the Times investigation)

"We had lists of the Subutex writers, and we were actively targeting them,"
– A former employee talking about doctors that prescribed generic Subutex.

In the United States, any physician who takes an eight-hour, online course about Suboxone can obtain authorization to prescribe it.

Most of these prescribers know very little about addiction; it's far out of the scope of their training and practice. In America, the majority of doctors prescribing Suboxone, have no training in addiction medicine. Most Suboxone doctors don't know how to get their clients off of the drug, as there is no protocol in place to do so. There have been no studies from the medical community on long-term effects of being on Suboxone or how to get a patient comfortably and safely off of it. You don't have to look to long or hard to find horror stories, and the obvious company advocates.

It seems that most doctors want to keep clients on the medication indefinitely, very few use it as a detoxification tool over four to six weeks, as it was designed. Suboxone's opioid component, buprenorphine, has a long half-life and tight adhesion to opiate receptors in the brain. Titration, reducing the dosage of Suboxone very slowly, allowing one, to two weeks for physical withdrawal symptoms, seems to be a popular opinion.

There are individuals who are addicted to Suboxone; I remember reading about one man's story of how he became addicted to Suboxone by starting out taking a small piece of his girlfriend's tablet. He had never done any other form of opiate, yet he ended up going to a Suboxone clinic to get his new drug of choice. Seven years later, he was ready to ask for help; imagine what he must have been thinking, and his fear.

Didn't we learn anything from the companies who produced the opiates that helped create the addiction problem that we have in America today while they filled their pockets with billions of dollars paid by the families who are now grieving their loved ones? The United States Market for Opioid Dependence is quickly approaching two billion dollars. Big Pharma, big business, and big dollars, when science and politics mix it must be for public welfare, not big business lining their pockets. They spent almost three billion lobbying the US Government in the past five years. Pharma is the king of all 121 lobbying entities and donated over $90 million to political parties and candidates. Gross annual earnings for Big Pharma was $950 billion plus globally.

The head of Nordic Cochrane Centre, Peter Gotzsche has written a book entitled: **Deadly Medicines and Organized Crime: How Big Pharma Has Corrupted Healthcare**. In the book, the author quotes a former vice-president of Pfizer as comparing Big Pharma to the mafia.

Morphine was created in 1817, codeine in 1832, heroin in 1874, OxyContin came to the United States in 1996.

Over the years with each drug, they were marketed as "thought to be less addicting" as the former. Statistics say that 95% of individuals trying to get off of Suboxone fail. Those who have been taking Suboxone for long periods of time are starting to ask troubling questions:

What about adrenal imbalances?
Is anyone else having psychological issues?
Is anyone else having hair loss?
Is anyone else losing teeth?
Is anyone having anxiety problems?
Is anybody having dissociative disorders?
Is anyone having endocrine system problems?
Are any ladies having premature menopause?
Do any guys have low testosterone?

The National Alliance of Advocates for Buprenorphine Treatment has started to post questionnaires on their website forums about these problems. If you have a problem with opiates, there's nothing wrong with Suboxone to aid your detox; however, be selective on who you go to get detoxed, or you may never get off of Suboxone. Be careful, you can get high on Suboxone, it dissolves in body fat and sticks to opiate receptors like cement! It seems that some doctors think that it's possible that Suboxone does more harm to the body than research has identified to date.

I went to a blog listed on N.A.A.B.T.'s website for Suboxone users listed are a few of the long-term users reported side effects:

Memory loss
Recall ability seriously impacted
High cognitive function impaired
Sex drive impaired
Emotions impaired
Bad headaches/ body twitching
Weight loss
Lack of motivation
Hair thinning

Stomach problems/ constipation
Ears ringing/ face numbness
Blurred vision
Depression and anger
Menstrual problems

Is Suboxone a terrible medication, probably not; the unknown seems to be the problem. Doctors who are going to prescribe Suboxone need to have more training on Suboxone and addiction then an eight-hour online course. There needs to be research into long-term effects of the use of these drugs and protocol to get people off of Suboxone after detoxification. We are in the middle of an opiate epidemic in this country that is killing our children every few minutes. Each has to weigh the information out for themselves and make the decision; is going on Suboxone better than the other choices available? For some individuals, the answer may be yes, for others no. I'm not here to make decisions for others, I know what I believe; however, ultimately the decision is yours. I hope this information helps you to make an informed decision on your journey to recovery.

Gabapentin is being used more and more frequently by individuals in methadone maintenance programs to get high; this can lead to injuries, accidents, and even death. Increasing availability, lack of infrequent drug screening, and potential of euphoria, when mixed with opioids, have all contributed to the misuse of gabapentin.

Dr. Joseph Insler was quoted as saying, "Increasing clinicians' understanding of this dilemma and focusing on good prescribing practices will improve clinical expertise, and patient care," The doctor, noted that gabapentin is usually not one of the drugs for which patients are tested in treatment programs.

Gabapentin in combination with a benzodiazepine, opiates, or even alcohol will potentiate the effect, and substance abusers look for the elevated high.

Often when substance abusers are going through the detox process they will experience insomnia and restless leg syndrome; gabapentin is often prescribed to deal with this problem. In extreme cases, individuals will experience seizures, gabapentin can sometimes be prescribed in these cases. No one knew that substance abusers could get high from or abuse this medication.

Resources

https://en.wikipedia.org/wiki/Buprenorphine
http://naabt.org/
Ask an Expert: Should I go Off Suboxone? If so, How? The Fix Dr. Richard Juman 4/29/15
The Suboxone Addict You Never Knew Existed. The Fix Daniel Mulligan 5/16/14
Treating Heroin Addicts with Suboxone Spurs Controversy. The Fix Brent McCluskey 12/09/14
So You Thought You Could Get Off Suboxone? The Fix Dawn Roberts 09/04/14
Big Pharma: Exposing the Global Healthcare Agenda Jacky Law 2/06/2006
http://www.suboxforum.com/stopping-suboxone.html
Deadly Medicines and Organized Crime, How Big Pharma Corrupted Healthcare Peter Gotzsche 2013
Trapped on Suboxone. The Fix Jennifer Matesa 12/02/13
Addiction with a Dark Side. New York Times Deborah Sontag 11/16/13
Drugs for Treating Heroin Users: A New Abuse Problem in The Making? The Christian Monitor Elizabeth Barber staff writer 5/20/2014
(A version of this article appears in print 11/17/13 The New York Addition R. R. Ruiz contributing reporter)
Clark, R. E., Baxter, J. D., Aweh, G., O'Connell, E., Fisher, W. H., & Barton, B. A. (2015). Risk Factors for Relapse and Higher Costs Among Medicaid Members with Opioid Dependence or Abuse: Opioid Agonists, Comorbidities, and Treatment History. J Subst Abuse Treat, 57, 75-80. doi: 10.1016/j.jsat.2015.05.001
Methadone: A Major Driver of Prescription Painkiller Overdose Deaths. The Fix Maia Szalavitz 7/03/2012

Harm reduction seems rather troubling in theory and practice. Why would we want to teach someone suffering from alcoholism or drug abuse to continue to use, but just use less? The toll that drugs and alcohol may have already taken on the person's health could be life threatening; any usage could be fatal, depending on the drug and the person. Ethically, how can we tell a person that it's all right to use illicit drugs? If the addiction "professional" understands addiction, they would understand that they are only dealing with a symptom here, not the root or the core of the problem. It would be a fool's game to think that those suffering from addiction haven't tried to use safely many times already and failed; that's why they need help in the first place. There is a good deal of merit to the statement, "a drug is a drug is a drug."

Faith-based programs can be effective; however, statistics are that only one per cent of people recover with religion alone. Faith-based programs in combination with twelve-step such as AA/ NA can be very effective. This type of model all depends on how the program is set up.

Holistic on its own is not very effective, other than to get the person in good shape. This too can become a much more effective program in combination with other programming. The substance abuser needs a vehicle to change addictive thinking and living. This will also depend on the components of the program.

Abstinence Models are good as long as they have vehicles for the substance abuser to change the way that they were living and thinking, such as twelve-step programs. Self-empowerment models are troubling because with most substance abusers and alcoholics, their best thinking and actions are what got them high and into the "jackpots" that they have suffered as a result of using.

> *"Changing is what people do when they have no options left."* –
> Holly Black

Common sense dictates that the same model will not work for every individual. There are many choices today including peer recovery coaches, professional recovery coaches, case managers, professional family recovery coaches, professional life coaches, interventionists, luxury treatment centers, therapists, counselors, Christian and Pastoral counselors, Al-anon, Families Anonymous, gambling addiction coaches, food addiction coaches, sexual addiction coaches, specialized treatment centers, community centers for recovery, all kinds of twelve-step meetings, sober companions, and much more. Each must choose what model works for them.

> *"Our greatest glory is not in never falling, but in rising every time we fall."* – Oliver Goldsmith

When you ask about success rates at treatment facilities, do you get a truthful answer? The complex answer here is yes and no. There is no concrete way for a facility to calculate their success rate. Think about it, if they stay in touch with former clients, how do they know if the former clients are honest with them or not? Clients move, change phone numbers, get married, change names, pass away, get unlisted numbers, etc. A facility may calculate their success rate out of the people who respond to them, or the former clients they are able to get in touch with. The question is, how accurate are these numbers? Some facilities consider their program a success if a client graduates their program. Some stay in touch for six months to a year. What standard are they measuring their success by?

Addiction is an epidemic in our nation. Our youth are dying every few minutes from substance abuse. There are all sorts of new drugs on the streets, new ways to make them and new ways to use them. Everyone must work together to stop the insanity, to stop the death. There are thousands of individuals in America with long-term recovery, they've been to Hell and made it back alive. There is no more time for anonymity when our young are dying in record numbers.

The solutions are already here, yet so many are trying to reinvent the wheel. America and the world are listening, it's time for those with long-term recovery to share the solutions that work!

Chapter Two A
Emerging Street Drugs

1. Heroin: This highly addictive opiate comes in a number of quantities, but we will focus on the individual dose, or "bag" and the "bundle". The "bag" in almost every situation is $10.00 worth of Heroin. To an active user two to three "bags" are needed per dose to give the user his/her desired high. The "bundle" is when the user buys "bags" in multiples of ten to usually get a better price per bag. Heroin can be ingested in three different ways: Snorting the drug is the least potent way to ingest Heroin and usually has the weakest withdrawals, which in turn makes it easier to hide the usage. Next, is Smoking the drug. Much like Cocaine, smoking Heroin gives the user a much more intense and rapid high. Last is the most potent and dangerous way to ingest Heroin and that is by injecting the drug directly into the bloodstream. The potency of Heroin varies so much that this makes injecting the drug extremely dangerous and the toll that injecting takes on the body makes it almost impossible to hide the usage. Prescription opiates have been popular for some time, as they become too expensive and harder to get, heroin has made a comeback. Studies have shown that over forty percent of teens don't think that using heroin once or twice a week is a major risk. On the street heroin is known as "H" or "Chiba or Chiva" or "Skag" or "Tar" among many other nicknames. It's killing our kids at a very rapid rate!

2. Cocaine: This highly addictive narcotic comes in a variety of different quantities as well, but we will focus on the individual doses that would relate to an "everyday user" as opposed to a dealer or trafficker. There are three very common quantities for the average Cocaine user and these would be a half gram, a gram and an 8-ball (3.5 grams). The price of these vary, but on average we are talking 25.00/30.00 per Half Gram, 50.00/60.00 per Gram and 150.00/200.00 per 8-Ball. Much like Heroin, Cocaine can be ingested in three different ways: Snorting is again the least potent way to ingest the drug and easiest to hide. It is also the most cost efficient way for the user to do the drug.

Next is Smoking Cocaine. This way of ingesting the drug gives the user a much more intense and rapid high than snorting and causes the user to go through much more of the drug in a short amount of time. And finally, there is injecting Cocaine. This way definitely gives the most intense high and is by far the most dangerous. Much like Heroin, the wear and tear that shooting Cocaine takes on the body is vicious and is extremely hard for the user to hide.

3. Meth: This drug is an extremely addictive amphetamine and comes in various amounts which are much smaller in quantity than Heroin or Cocaine. Meth, known as "the poor man's Cocaine" is extremely potent and is only needed in smaller amounts. The smallest is the "point" which is actually only 1/10th of a gram and costs the user about $10.00. Next is the "quarter" which is exactly that…. a ¼ gram and usually costs the user $25.00. A "gram" of Meth runs about $100.00 and a "teener" costs about $175.00 and is 1/16 of an Ounce. All of these prices are easily attainable for the average person, but the use of this drug is the hardest to hide from friends and family because of the toll that it takes on the body, especially the skin. Once of the biggest signs of Meth abuse is open sores appearing on the body (especially the face) from the user picking obsessively while being high. Methamphetamine is a neurotoxin that used to be very difficult to make, not anymore there is a new more dangerous process! On the street, it is known as "rolling the bottle" it's the new one pot meth labs. It can be made just about anywhere using chemicals from the pharmacy and a small bottle. It is very dangerous! The bottle has to be opened just at the right time during the process, if not it can catch on fire, explode and release harmful ammonia gasses. The pharmacies don't communicate with each other on who purchases the necessary chemicals to create the end product. Meth is a horrible, destructive drug that takes and takes until nothing is left. Not even one shred of hope will be left by the time meth eats through a life, a soul, or a family.

Meth is patient, cunning, and extremely ruthless as it melts a person's dreams, opportunities, and soul like acid. Heroin is cheap and it kills quickly. Meth is cheap and it creates zombies that eventually go quiet and still.

4. Roxicodone/Oxycontin: This section should be a seminar all on its own. The newest epidemic is actually prescribed by Doctors at an alarming rate and sold illegally on the streets in large amounts. These pills can be swallowed, snorted or injected. Not only are these pills single-handedly destroying lives, they are also directly responsible for a "spin-off" heroin epidemic. With the government cracking down and restricting the manufacturing of these pills the illegal street price had gone from $8.00 a pill (30 mg) to $25.00 a pill (30 mg) in less than one year. Before we get into the quantities and signs of abuse, let's make sure we know the difference between the two widely abused pills. Roxicodone pills come in 15 mgs and 30 mgs and are immediate release pain pills used to fight severe pain. The 30 mgs are usually baby blue in color, but new lighter blue (almost white) are starting to surface. The 15 mgs are always light green in color. The 15 mgs are now $12.00 while the 30 mgs run $25.00. To the average user (2) 30 mg pills are needed to obtain the "abusers" high. Now, oxycontin is a "controlled release" pill meaning that oxycodone is time released into the body over a long period of time…oxycodone is the shared opiate between the two pills we are discussing, roxicodone and oxycontin. Many people think they are the same pill but remember, roxicodone(roxy) is immediate release while oxycontin(oxy) is time released…So you can see where the "immediate need addict" usually prefers the roxy. We mentioned earlier that these pills were contributing to a "spin-off" Heroin epidemic. Like we stated before, in less than one year the illegal street price of a Roxy has gone from $8.00 to $25.00 due to new restrictions by the government on prescriptions and manufacturing of the pill while the cost of a single bag of Heroin has stayed at $10.00. Both Heroin and Roxicodone are Opiates and produce the same effect and feeling for the user.

So with the cost of a Roxy skyrocketing, users are beginning to revert to the more cost efficient Heroin. Which, in turn, is creating a whole new Heroin epidemic.

5. Xanax/Klonopin: The benzodiazepine crowd of drugs is usually prescribed from a doctor and starts off with a client's chief complaint of 'anxiety that not which is specified." A PHD or MD will give a client a dose of these to 'calm them' with instructions usually before bed and Per Diem, meaning as needed. What happens with a client is the 'anxiety', real or imagined gives the addict a crutch or excuse to get high. "Because the doctor gave it to me and it is legal it is okay," is what most clients rely on when wanting to use. The drugs are physically and mentally addictive and the client begins to use more than what was originally given and seek them on the street. Can be taken orally but more commonly crushed and snorted or shot with a needle. Sometimes paired with cocaine to remove the paranoia. Pills can sell for as low as $7.00 a pill up to $15 or $20 depending on the area.

6. Adderall/Paxil: These uppers are usually given to clients with ADD or ADHD and the client will usually take them orally or crush them and snort them or even shoot them. If a client has ADD or ADHD, the drugs will calm them down and help them focus. If the client does not, the client will get a rush or feel a speed effect. Sometimes these drugs are paired with Benzos or opiates for a 'speed ball' effect.

7. Ecstasy's and Molly: "E" and Molly are known party drugs. Clients will go to clubs or Rave's or Ultra Music Fest and take these party drugs to 'roll'. The drugs give the client a warm fuzzy happy feeling and increase the sense of touch, sight, smell, and sound. The client is fairly docile and will ingest or snort the drugs. They sell anywhere from $10.00 a pill to $20.00 depending on location and event. Clients usually do not overdose or die on these drugs, they usually dehydrate because they forget to drink water and can end up in the ER or dead. Molly, slang for "molecular" referring to the pure crystalline powder from the club drug in pill form ecstasy.

It's supposed to be MDMA but it's not, the real chemicals are running short, so in China, dealers are creating fake MOLLY made with all different substitute chemicals and poisons.

Crime labs in South Florida tested some of the street Molly and found that it contained Methylone, a dangerous chemical found in "Bath Salts!" Users are risking their lives anytime they take this Mystery Molly! All these chemicals are very dangerous! Once Molly enters the bloodstream doctors may not be able to reverse the damages done by the unknown poisons. This drug is also killing our kids!

8. Special K (Ketamine): Horse Tranquilizer. Usually snorted or mixed with other assorted drugs. Sometimes shot. Usually bought on the black market. The Pill is sold on market value.

9. PCP/LSD/Mushrooms: Can be on paper, in pill, liquid or other forms. Mushrooms 'shrooms' look like freeze-dried mushrooms and can be eaten or make into a tea to drink. Psychedelics cause a 'tripping' effect. Price varies depending on location. Usually as cheap as 10.00 and can last up to twelve hrs.

10. Krokodil: Is a synthetic "heroin-like" drug called Desomorphine that is made by combining codeine tablets with toxic industrial chemicals and lighter fluid. It is known for destroying the flesh of the user. Another killer!

11. "N-Bomb": Refers to any three closely related synthetic hallucinogens that are being sold as legal substitutes for LSD or Mescaline. "Legal Acid," "Smiles," and "251" are nicknames for the drug. It can be in a powder form or a liquid soaked into blotter paper (like LSD) or in food. More powerful than LSD ever has been and more dangerous! It is causing seizures, heart attacks, and deaths!

12. "Syrup," "Purple Drank," "Sizzurp": or "Lean"- really hits home for me as I lost a friend to this drug a few months ago. Prescription strength cough syrup containing codeine and promethazine mixed with soda, and sometimes hard candies.

Codeine and other opioids present a high risk of fatal overdose due to their effect of depressing the central nervous system, which can slow or stop the heart and lungs. Mixing with alcohol greatly increases this risk. Deaths are happening, and will continue!

13. "Shatter": Is frozen hash oil. Some call it wax or weed wax. Very powerful can be sixty to ninety percent THC, compared to a normal joint on average is twenty percent THC. Making this product is very dangerous, can cause explosions and fires!

14. "Flakka": Is an amphetamine, just like Molly. This synthetic stimulant contains alpha –PVP which was banned and labeled a schedule 1 drug by the US DEA in 2014 the drug has flooded the South Florida, Texas, and Ohio areas. It initially increases dopamine, the brain's pleasure chemical, you become alert and euphoric. The side effects are aggression, irregular heartbeat, seizures, hallucinations, delusions, and death.

15. Bath salts: A legal substance that heats the brain up and clouds it at the same time. Can be bought at local gas stations for $5.00 and lasts all day. Designed to mimic cocaine. Snorted, cooked and smoked or shot.

16. Smiles: Designed to mimic Meth, again totally legal and sold at gas stations, head shops. Snorted, cooked and smoked, or shot. $3-5 lasts all day.

17. Spice: Synthetic Marijuana, can be rolled with or without tobacco and smoked. DOES NOT SMELL LIKE MJ. This label on the package says "potpourri' and not for human consumption. Yet the clients will take it. $5.00 lasts all day. Very Dangerous!

18. W-18: A powerful white powder being shipped from China may be more deadly than heroin! In the 1980s, scientists at the University of Alberta developed W-18, a synthetic opiate that produces a high like heroin.

W-18 is 100 times stronger than Fentanyl and 10,000 times more potent than Morphine; it was developed as a potential painkiller, there are thirty strains in the W series, W-18 is the strongest. No tests are available to detect the presence of W-18 in blood or urine.

19. Everyday More Illicit Drugs are created that can injure or kill our children. Please stay informed.

(Information gathered from Wikipedia.)

Chapter Three
The Disease Model of Addiction & The Twelve-Step Modality of Recovery

The disease of addiction, it starts with the big lie that allows addicts to use again despite all the negative consequences that have happened as a result of using, this is centered in the mind. This is called the mental obsession, or the disease of the mind. Then the addict puts the chemicals into their body, and they lose the power of choice. This is called the phenomenon of craving, or allergy, or allergy defined, abnormal reaction. Addiction in its simplest term is a living and a thinking problem, or lack of power. Drugs and alcohol are but a symptom of the problem. The disease of the mind coupled with the disease of the body then leads to hopelessness or a malady of the spirit. The problem defines the solution, so the solution must be power. The addict needs to change the way that they think and live. They need an entire psychic change. (Process addictions are behavior addictions such as pathological gambling and sexual addiction.)

The individual suffering from addiction has a blocked spirit or self-centeredness at the center of the person where spirit should be in a normal person. Because the spirit is blocked, this causes the basic instincts to become out of balance, such as sexual, social, and security. The individual then will experience fears, resentments, and personal harms to self and others as the disease progresses.

Self-centeredness is at the root of addiction and shame is at the core of addiction.

The goal of the twelve-step process is for the individual to live a spirit-centered life once again and have the basic instincts become balanced, eliminating the fears, resentments, and harms caused by addiction. The ultimate goal is more than sobriety, it's about change.

(The Twelve Steps are broken down into simple form.)

Step 1 Gives us the problem
Step 2 Gives us the solution
Step 3 A decision to live in the solution
Steps 4 through 9 Action steps
Steps 10 through 12 Continued growth & maintenance

A program of recovery provides a vehicle to change. A fellowship supports that change. The program of recovery or vehicle would come from the basic textbook and the fellowship and support come from the meeting. This modality of recovery requires complete abstinence from illicit drugs and alcohol. The result of working the program of recovery is an entire psychic change. The addict is essentially reborn.

The twelve-step modality is not the only way to recover from the disease of addiction. There are many modalities to treat addiction. If you or a loved one is caught in the grips of addiction right now, please get help. Don't let this cunning, baffling, and powerful disease take another life. Do all that you can to get between your loved one and the disease. As long as there is life, there is hope! You are not alone on this journey. Whoever you are, parent, student, teacher, addict, son or daughter, friend, there is support for you. Knowledge is power. The truth shall set us free!

In January 2016, ASAM released a new definition of addiction that involved eighty experts over a four-year process. The new definition is as follows: Addiction is a brain disorder, not a behavior issue. Addiction is a chronic brain disorder and not simply a behavior problem involving alcohol, drugs, gambling or sex; experts contend in a new definition of addiction, one that is not solely related to problematic substance abuse.

What Is Addiction?

There are many thoughts on what the problem of addiction is. A quick Google search yields 161,000,000 results. I looked up ten different places, and these are the results.

1. In 1934, William D. Silkworth M.D. attended a patient who was alcoholic. Dr. Silkworth said, "I had come to regard him as hopeless." Dr. Silkworth wrote the chapter in ***"The Big Book" of Alcoholics*** Anonymous known as "The Doctor's Opinion." In this chapter, the doctor describes alcoholism as a disease of the mind due to the mental obsession. Combined with a disease of the body, because of the phenomenon of craving or allergy, or allergy defined is an abnormal reaction."
2. In 1956, The American Medical Association had declared that alcoholism was an illness.
3. In 1991, The AMA further endorsed the dual classification of alcoholism by the International Classification of Diseases under both psychiatric and medical sections.
4. In 2004, The World Health Organization stated that alcoholism is a brain disorder.
5. The American Society of Addiction Medicine and the AMA both maintain that alcoholism is a disease.
6. NAADAC: The Association for Addiction Professionals believes that Science has shown that addiction is a brain disease that responds well to treatment.
7. The Recovery Community, those in long-term recovery believe that alcoholism is a disease as described by Dr. Silkworth.
8. The Faith-based community is divided some believe that alcoholism is a disease; some believe it's a sin.
9. Most clinicians believe that addiction is a brain disorder.
10. The ASAM defines addiction: as a *"primary, chronic disease of the brain with characteristic biological, psychological, social and spiritual manifestations."*

"The man takes a drink or drug, the drink takes a drink (The drug takes a drug), the drink or drug takes the man!" Author Unknown

If you genuinely want to solve the problem, then you can find a solution to anything; there are perception and perspective problems in most cases, though. There are also many opinions about what the solution to addiction is. There are many modalities to choose from. Different treatment models teach different programs based on what they believe. Some let the client choose what modality they will follow.

It's a mixed bag. There are so many theories by many different types of people.

- *Medical community members: doctors, clinicians, and scientists*
- *The faith-based community of the Reverends, Rabbis, Yogis, and healers.*
- *Twelve-step community, and grassroots programs*
- *Secular recovery*
- *Some addicts rely on self-help*

The types of treatment, support, and help have expanded over the years to include:

- *Harm Reduction, Emotional Intelligence, Cognitive Behavioral Therapy,*
- *Neuroscience, Motivational Interviewing,*
- *Inpatient, Outpatient, Aftercare, Medication Assisted Treatment, Detox,*
- *Recovery Coaching, Family Recovery Coaching,*
- *Interventions, Sober Companions, Sponsors, Peer Mentors,*
- *Therapy, Counseling,*
- *Sober Housing, Residential Treatment*

Help – Expert or Experienced?

Think about this logically for a moment. We are certainly dealing with life and death, so every decision is very important.

Let's say you were going to a place that you had never been, a very dangerous place! For our purposes here we will say that you are on a reality TV show, and you have to spend the weekend in the Everglades in Florida.

Let me ask you a question: Would you rather go for the weekend with a guide that had read a book about the Everglades and had some theories, or would you rather go with a guide that had been there many times and made it back alive and was a tried, tested, and proven guide? I think the correct answer is clear.

The recovery community looks at drugs and alcohol as a symptom of the problem, not the problem.

If you take the alcohol away from an alcoholic, they still have all of the isms. They will still have the living and the thinking problem that needs to change. They will need a vehicle to change and a support system to support that vehicle. No magic pill is ever going to work as the answer to addiction. The problem defines the solution.

Addressing the underlying causes and core issues of addiction means, that in most cases, the symptoms go away. We're talking about self-centeredness and shame here as the root and the core of addiction. Living a spirit-centered life will deal with both of these issues.

Addicts and alcoholics need a way to identify and understand the problem that they have so that they can admit and accept that they have it. A solution to solve the problem and a decision that they want to solve it. They will need an action plan or road map to get there, and a plan to maintain their freedom so that they can continue to grow in spirituality. With incentive, support, and directions, the alcoholic or addict will go from harmful self or self-centered to spirit-centered.

There may also be underlying or co-occurring problems that will also need to be dealt with by a professional. There may be physical problems, living-skills problems, emotional problems, mental health problems, spiritual problems, etc.

"Obviously, you don't go to the dentist when you hurt your knee! The person needs to get help from the proper professional or professionals." – Rev. Kev.

What Is Recovery?

Again, the perceptions and definitions of recovery vary, depending on the beliefs surrounding the addition. Some believe that recovery requires total abstinence from all mood altering substances while others do not.

A recent study, "What is Recovery?" is a project of the Alcohol Research Group and offers answers from individuals in recovery and describes their personal definitions. Beyond those personal references are scientific, medical, spiritual, secular and Twelve-step based definitions:

- *"Recovery is a daily reprieve contingent upon the maintenance of one's spiritual condition."* –*AA Basic Text*

- There are many different pathways to recovery
- Recovery is self-directed and empowering
- Recovery involves a personal recognition of the need for change
- The root of addiction is self-centeredness, shame is at the core
- Recovery is holistic
- Recovery has many cultural dimensions
- Recovery exists on a continuum of improvement in wellness and overall health
- Recovery is born of gratitude and hope
- Recovery is a process of self-discovery and healing
- Recovery has several support systems
- Recovery involves a process of rebuilding and re-establishing a life and community

It's clear that even if the definitions of addiction or recovery differ, all believe that recovery is possible and a fact. Understanding the Problem and Creating a Solution.

Support Groups for Families:

Families Anonymous: (FA) is a twelve-step program for relatives and friends of addicts. FA was founded in 1971 by a group of parents in Southern California concerned with their children's substance abuse. As of 2007, there are FA meetings in more than twenty countries and about two hundred and twenty-five regular meetings in the United States. The focus of FA is on supporting members rather than changing the behavior of their friend or relative with a substance abuse problem.

Tough love is suggested as an approach to use when dealing with addicts—members do not need to rescue addicts from the consequences of problems the addicts have created, and members should be willing to offend addicts if necessary. (From Wikipedia)

Al-Anon: defines itself as an independent fellowship with the stated purpose of helping relatives and friends of alcoholics. Al-Anon holds the view that alcoholism is a family illness. The Al-Anon Family Groups are a fellowship of relatives and friends of alcoholics who share their experience, strength, and hope in order to solve their common problems. They believe alcoholism is a family illness and that changed attitudes can aid recovery. (From Wikipedia)

Chapter Four
Meet the Professional Recovery Coach

Becoming a professional coach doesn't happen overnight. It takes a particular type of person and personality to be a professional coach. It takes a lifetime of training to get the skills, tools, and wisdom to be a professional coach. You can't just attend a coaching school for a few days or weeks and be a professional coach; it takes much more.

To be a coach you have to enjoy working with people, be an excellent listener, and like to help solve problems. It seems that those who are spiritual make stronger coaches. There are many niches within the coaching industry. Professional coaches don't have to be able to coach in every niche; however, they do need to master the niche that they wish to work within. "You can comfort where you have been comforted." In other words, it's best to coach in an arena that you know and have a plethora of experience in. The best professional coaches have had success within the arena that they are coaching in.

Professional coaches are not therapists or counselors. Coaches don't do any process work; looking into the client's past to help find a solution. Coaching is client and results driven; you could say that coaching is a very advanced form of encouragement. Everything is generated from the client; the coach must be very careful not to cross the fine line that separates coaching from other practices that require licensing. This becomes a matter of ethics and training, if a new coach follows the necessary eleven core competencies, they should stay out of harm's way along these lines.

One of the most challenging niches is Professional Recovery Coaching, especially when it comes to letting the client drive the plan. This can be a real catch twenty-two; how can a person with a thinking problem make good choices? Recovery coaches have to be very creative to operate within the boundaries of the law.

"A good coach asks great questions to help you remove the obstacles in your mind and to get you back on track in life." – Farshad Asl

What is a Professional Recovery Coach? Is it an AA sponsor? Don't be mistaken! These Professional Addiction Recovery Coaches are highly trained, very skilled, knowledgeable, educated, and experts in their respective fields. Various individuals seem to think that these coaches are just recovering alcoholics and former substance abusers that are like AA sponsors, that couldn't be farther from reality! These Professional Coaches are experts! Professional Recovery Coaches have to be the best in their field because they're not dealing with a failing business; they're dealing with a failing life! The stakes couldn't be higher for these pros!

Who started recovery coaching? Bob Timmons, a California-based addiction specialist, is recognized as introducing recovery coaching into the mainstream in 1986. He assisted a famous rock band in finding sobriety from heroin addiction.

Professional Recovery Coaches will go to events with the client, or stay with the client for a period of time to help them get through a difficult period in their lives. Clients can also see professional coaches by the hour during weekly sessions. There is also peer recovery coaching.

Professional Recovery Coaches receive professional training that involves certain competencies such as ethics, action planning, active listening, powerful questioning, legal responsibilities, and referral through disengagement, interactive and written testing, and much more. Professional-recovery coaching is a client and results driven service that is a form of strengths-based support for those persons with addictions, or in recovery from alcohol or drug dependence, process addictions, codependency, and other addictive behaviors.

There are many schools of thought as to life coaching philosophy.

Each coach will develop their own philosophy as they train, learn, and practice their craft. Successful coaches develop their own niche of expertise in coaching. Some coaches specialize in business coaching, other fitness coaching, career coaching, financial coaching, relationship coaching, and recovery coaching. There are many other types of coaching as well.

Today there are coaching specializations within the niche of professional coaching. For example, within the field of professional recovery coaching, there is family recovery coaching, gambling addiction coaching, sex addiction coaching, and others. There are many training courses offered to train coaches on these specialty niches in different training organizations.

Professional-recovery coaches do not diagnose, provide primary treatment, and don't subscribe to any particular modality of treatment. The coaches don't deal with any mental-health issues. They don't do therapy or any form of counseling. Professional-recovery Coaching is action oriented, emphasizing improving present life and achieving future goals.

It seems like every week there is a new emerging drug on the streets that can kill our kids. Approximately every two minutes another young person dies from addiction. Every week science finds some new evidence to deal with addiction. Every month or two a new modality pops up to help people recover from addiction. From engagement through disengagement, the coach has to help differentiate the true from the false. Not an easy task at all! Research has shown the importance of long-term aftercare to successful long-term sobriety.

Insurance does not cover recovery coaching; however, most believe in the future that will change. The cost for Professional Recovery Coaches depends on the experience of the coach and the location.

Fees can range from seventy-five dollars per hour to five-hundred dollars per hour depending on the coach or company. These professionals are well worth their fees.

In a world where most avenues to stop the disease of addiction have failed, Professional Recovery Coaching is an exciting new field that seems to be very effective in reaching solutions for long-term recovery in assisting those who were once lost to addiction find hope.

Chapter Five
Co-dependency, Enabling and the Family

For more than nineteen years now I have been the Director of a residential drug and alcohol recovery facility in Northeastern Pennsylvania. I have a great deal of experience with addiction and recovery, families, and the twelve-step process. My first experience with addiction was the death of my uncle in the Bowery from alcoholism; unfortunately, he never experienced the program of Alcoholics Anonymous. My mother who was one of the co-founders of the facility took me to AA meetings from the age of seven. She had over forty years of sobriety when she passed a few years ago. I loved going to meetings with my mom when I was a boy and listening to the speakers tell their stories. I didn't care for the step meetings too much back then. Sure enough, I turned out to be an alcoholic and took my lumps for a few years.

My family dropped me off in treatment. I called home once a week. They visited me after thirty days. They didn't interfere with the treatment plan, or try to tell the professionals how to do their jobs. They knew that they had left me in good hands, so they trusted them to do their job. They did! I failed the first two times there, but it wasn't the program's fault or the facility's fault. It was my fault! I didn't do what they taught me to do! The third time around, I was serious! I did everything they told me to do. It worked, and it's still working almost two decades later! I don't know why people blame the program or facility for failing when the client just didn't work the program.

One of the biggest problems that interrupts treatment plans is enabling by the families. They love their kids and want to believe them, but how can they believe their substance abuser over the treatment professionals? We even coach families on what their loved ones might say or do at certain points of their recovery. Some of the families still enable their kids! It's quite amazing! They are helping to kill their kids.

If you have a substance abuser in the family, and you can't figure out who the enabler in the family is, it's you! The good news is that you can hire a professional family recovery coach that will only work with the family. You can also hire a professional recovery coach that will only work with the substance abuser. There is nothing like knowledge and experience to help empower people. The other good news is that the recovery process works. If someone wants to recover from addiction they can.

There are new modalities, medicines, and ideas popping up all the time. That being said, the families can make a huge impact by not enabling and learning all that they can about addiction and recovery. Support recovery, but do not enable, it kills! I won't even disclose how many poor souls that I have known have lost their lives to addiction that may be alive today if enabling were not involved. Ultimately you have to put the blame on the person who chooses to use drugs or alcohol if they know that they have a problem; however, when you add an enabler to the picture, it's like adding TNT!

The Enabler: This person will minimize the substance abuser's behavior, make excuses for him or her and provide money, services for the substance abuser. This person plays the martyr role and usually complains that the addict is not getting better but will be the first person to refuse to cut off ties with the addict and continues to send money or items to allow the addict to continue using substances. This person will interrupt the recovery plan. Take the addict out of programs, believe the lies and manipulations of the substance abuser.

This behavior must be stopped! Enabling, an active substance abuser or an abuser in early recovery, always apply this rule: If their lips are moving, they are probably lying! Don't believe the lies and manipulations.

Support recovery, but don't enable. When they go to Detox and Residential Programs, when they want to use or leave, they will say anything to get out.

Common excuses: they're mean to me, there's no food, they're not giving me anything to drink, it's dirty, the food is awful, there is no program here, everyone is having sex, everyone is getting high here, the counselor said I'm ready to leave, there's no staff here, they stole my money, I don't want you to pay for me anymore, whatever it is that they think will push your buttons and get to you as parents!

Listen to the professionals; that's what you are paying them for. Enabling: is a term with a double meaning in psychotherapy and mental health.

As a positive term, enabling references patterns of interaction which allow individuals to develop and grow. These patterns may be on any scale, for example within the family, or in wider society as "Enabling acts" designed to empower some group, or create a new authority for a (usually governmental) body. When we talk about enabling in regards to addiction, it is in a negative sense.

*In a negative sense, enabling is also used to describe dysfunctional behavior approaches that are intended to help resolve a specific problem but, in fact, may perpetuate or exacerbate the problem. A common theme of enabling in this latter sense is that third parties take responsibility, blame, or make accommodations for a person's harmful conduct (often with the best of intentions, or from fear or insecurity which inhibits action).

The practical effect is that the person himself or herself does not have to do so, and is shielded from awareness of the harm it may do, and the need or pressure to change. Enabling in this sense is a major environmental cause of addiction.

A common example of enabling can be observed in the relationship between the alcoholic/addict and a codependent spouse.

The spouse who attempts to shield the addict from the negative consequences of their behavior by calling in sick to work for them, making excuses that prevent others from holding them accountable, and cleaning up the mess that occurs in the wake of their impaired judgment. In reality, what the spouse is doing may be hurting, not helping. Enabling can tend to prevent psychological growth in the person being enabled, and can contribute to negative symptoms in the enabler.

One of the primary reasons for a formal Family Intervention with alcoholics/addicts is to help the family cease their enabling behaviors.

Tough love: Is an expression used, usually for the purpose of justification, when someone treats another person harshly or sternly with the intent to help them in the long run. The phrase was evidently coined by Bill Milliken when he wrote the book Tough Love in 1968 and has been used by numerous authors since then.

Tough love is still about love; it's about making tough choices to help someone who you care about in the long run. For example, genuinely concerned parents refusing to support their drug-addicted child financially until he or she enters drug rehabilitation would be said to be practicing tough love. Athletic coaches who maintain strict rules and highly demanding training regimens, but who care about their players, could also be said to be practicing tough love.

"Tough love" boot camps for teenagers have been described as child abuse, and the National Institutes of Health noted that "get tough treatments do not work, and there is some evidence that they may make the problem worse." When we use the term "Tough Love" we simply mean, support recovery, don't enable addiction, set boundaries, take care of yourself, get support.

To clarify, when we talk about tough love when it comes to addiction, it means support recovery; however, don't enable addictive behaviors in any way shape, or form.

Codependency

(Usually the Enabler but can be any of the family roles)
Definition (this is not mental health but a socially learned behavior)

The Enabler is usually your Codependent Personality and will attempt to sabotage the substance abuser consciously or subconsciously. The Co-Dependent will put their needs first, above the substance abuser and will expect someone else to understand their plight and solve all the issues but at the same time not make any changes. To be successful you will need to:

1. **Set a firm boundary with the codependent personality.**
2. **Set clear expectations with the codependent personality.**
3. **Use the family as a buffer between the codependent and the substance abuser.**

Codependency has become the buzzword for relationships and more when talking about someone with an addiction. Most people who suffer from addictions are codependent. Those in a relationship who try to control the behavior of a partner face frustration, rage, hopelessness and despair. The inability to separate themselves psychologically from others in their lives causes real emotional problems and leaves codependents vulnerable to enormous pain. Codependency is a learned behavior that is often from a generational cycle. It is an emotional and behavioral condition that affects an individual's ability to have healthy, mutually satisfying relationships. It is also sometimes called "relationship addiction" because people with codependency often form or maintain relationships that are one-sided, emotionally destructive and or abusive.

Codependents have low self-esteem and look for anything externally to feel better. They have difficulty feeling normal. Some use of substances such as alcohol, drugs or nicotine—and become addicted.

Others may develop compulsive behaviors like:
- Work-a-holism
- Gambling
- Indiscriminate sexual activity
- Hoarding
- Shopping addictions
- Constant complaining
- Constant caretaking
- Excessive animals

Codependent people have good intentions. Codependents view themselves as victims and are attracted to that same weakness in their relationships and friendships.

Roles that Codependents will play:

In relationships, codependents assume a variety of roles that protect their illusions and keep them in a relationship:

- The Rescuer
- The caretaker
- The Joiner
- The Hero
- The Complainer
- The Adjuster

The most common characteristics of Codependents?

1. Excessive caretaking
2. Low self-esteem
3. Denial
4. Fear of anger
5. Health problems
6. Addictive behaviors

Characteristics of Codependents will display:

- An exaggerated sense of responsibility for the actions of other people.

- A tendency to confuse love and pity, with the tendency to "love" people they can pity and rescue.
- A tendency to do more than their share, all of the time, and to become hurt when People don't recognize their efforts.
- An unhealthy dependence on relationships. The codependent will do anything to hold on to a relationship in order to avoid the feeling of abandonment.
- An extreme need for approval and recognition
- A sense of guilt when asserting themselves
- A compelling need to control other people around them
- Lack of trust in self or other people
- Fear of being abandoned

Remember, don't enable addictive behaviors any longer; however, support efforts for recovery from addiction.

Chapter Six
Helping Parents of Substance Abusers Deal with Misdirected Anger

"They can't treat our son like that, even if he is an addict, we're suing!" Johnny slept with three females in the treatment center, checked medication and stockpiled pills so that he could get high, was late to meetings every day, lied to staff, gossiped about everyone, created trouble every day, threatened staff, and stole money and cigarettes from other clients before being terminated from the treatment program he was in. He was at the residential facility for eight days before they asked him to leave. Johnny should have been terminated on his first day when he threatened a staff member, behavior such as this should never be tolerated! The sad truth is that the parents still don't blame Johnny for his actions or hold him accountable; there must be consequences for all actions. The parents have blinders on, blaming the treatment center and enabling Johnny ultimately helping to kill him.

Anger comes from hurt and fear. Any parent with an addicted child suffers an unimaginable and torturous existence waiting for the call. The police, the hospital, a friend, who will call with the news that their child is dead or in jail? Every few minutes another young person's heart stops because of their battle with addiction and their parent's hearts are forever broken. The fear for parents is extremely justified and very real. Their anger, resentment, and rage are also very real. The problem is they get angry at the wrong person, place, or thing. They should be angry at addiction, not the treatment center and not Johnny. If Johnny was diabetic and had an episode would they punish him, of course not. Addiction is a disease, not a choice.

Johnny's parents should be thanking the treatment center for not enabling him. The only way that he can move forward is with honesty. A house built on quicksand cannot stand! You have to build recovery upon a solid foundation of truth and honesty.

Because the parents are in pain they have to do something with that pain, so they play the blame game. Misdirected anger comes shooting out their mouths and the tips of their pointer fingers.

> **"It's your faults!"**
> **"You didn't help our son."**
> **"He wants to go to an IOP."**
> **"There's no counseling."**

"He said that you were mean to him, that the food was bad, everyone was having sex, the meetings were boring, he wasn't getting anything out of the meetings, people were getting high, and he doesn't need residential."

If Johnny's lips are moving, you can bet he is manipulating! The parents can't see the forest through the trees because of misdirected anger; they're blind to the truth. There is no way that a treatment center can allow one person to interrupt or interfere with the recovery of others in the facility. The staff must protect the whole, just like the shepherd protects the flock. It's not that the life of every sheep isn't very important, but the whole comes first.

The parents need family recovery coaching and AMA or APA training and anger management to help them deal with their addicted loved one. It will also aid the family to attend fellowships such as Families Anonymous or Al-Anon which have programs that promote change within the family and coping skills. There are anger management practitioners around the country that can help parents deal with misdirected anger and teach them the warning signs and symptoms and coping mechanisms. The treatment center can prepare the family for some of the problems that can arise with their loved one. Many good treatment centers have family programs to avoid manipulations and bad behaviors by the addicted family member and helps to provide coping skills to the family.

It's really sad that people who give their very lives to helping to save the lives of others often get blamed for the bad behaviors of the same people that they are trying to help because of the misdirected parental anger. Imagine how frustrating it is for someone who gives their all to fight this terrible and deadly disease only to be blamed by an angry parent because their adult child manipulated them. It becomes a distraction and a no win situation for anyone. Parents need to think things through, and treatment centers need to prepare parents so that misdirected anger can be identified and defused.

The message for parents is that you hired the professionals for a reason; they are the professionals, let them do their jobs. Don't bite the bullet of manipulation any longer. We know that you love your son or daughter, that's why we do what we do! We want them to stay alive and have wonderful, long, any happy lives with you. Trust is so important in relationships! It is paramount in any relationship. The truth leads to freedom and professionals are ethically bound, to be honest. When the curtain goes up, and the smoke and mirrors come out, it's your addict driving the bus of manipulation, no one else. "Think, think, think!" Always think things through when it comes to your addicted loved one, always verify facts with a third party, use your common sense, don't react on emotion.

Remember parents, you are not alone in this war! You have a great deal of support to help you and your loved one. We are an army who are well-trained professionals to fight this cunning, baffling, and powerful enemy to help save the life of your loved one and help give you peace. There is nothing we love more than knowing that your loved one is safe, in recovery, and for the first time in months, you're not waiting for "the call", and you can rest soundly. We are here for you and your family!

Chapter Seven
Dual Diagnosis

I noticed quite a few years ago that suddenly everyone in early recovery from addiction to drugs and alcohol was also being diagnosed as bipolar; not just a few people, almost everyone was being given this label. Most of these individuals were also taking medications that their doctor had prescribed to deal with their mania and depression. Suddenly everyone had a "dual diagnosis," these seemed like magical words for managed-care approvals.

Most of the thousands and thousands of substance abusers in early recovery that I have crossed paths with over the past four decades have had a great deal of trouble understanding who they are early on in their sobriety. One common factor that all substance abusers share in early recovery is a certain level of situational depression from living in the hopelessness of addiction. I couldn't help but think: How can a doctor know who the real person is if the real person doesn't even know who they are?

In recovery people start to come back to life at approximately the six-month mark; they seem to have real clarity at that point, and the real person comes out of the darkness. The problem with diagnosing mental health illness in early recovery before this period is the overlap in symptoms of several mental health conditions that would seem reasonable but which, however, may well be false. The real person can't possibly be known when someone is impacted by the process of withdrawing from their drug of choice and learning to cope with life without it. A person may also experience mental-health symptoms from post-acute withdrawal syndrome anywhere from six to eighteen months after withdrawal.

A few years ago, I learned about the problem-solving principle of Occam's Razor.

The theory defined in simple terms: when you have competing hypotheses, the one that makes the fewest assumptions is most likely to be the most accurate and should be selected.

Certainly anyone who has just hit bottom is going to be depressed; why wouldn't they be? Self-centeredness is the root of addiction and shame is at the core. Fear, harm and resentment all grow as instincts fall out of balance because the addicted person's spirit is blocked by harmful self or self-centeredness. In early recovery as people face their fears, and stop lying and manipulating, they learn about the process of change through honesty, humility, willingness, and open-mindedness. When the mirror is held up to a recovering person's face for the first time in years, of course, they will feel some depression.

Every alcoholic and drug abuser who I have met knows anger. Born from hurt and fear, anger is normal for people in early recovery to feel and deal with on a daily basis. Most individuals I've talked with in recovery tell me at one point early on they were suicidal. Many in recovery have shared with me that they would tell their families that they were suicidal to manipulate them to get what they wanted from them. None of them committed suicide; it was just thoughts and feelings, an emotional roller-coaster!

The big question then becomes: Is the person's depression because of a problem with their brain chemistry, or is it situational because of life choices? Common sense dictates that the way to find out is to make a better life choice and see if the depression gets better, if it doesn't, the answer is clear. To medicate prior to investigation seems like insanity to me. The problem in the first place could be that the individual has been self-medicating if it is brain chemistry that's causing the depression. The only way to find the truth is when the person is back to baseline, the real, raw person.

These predetermined labels can be very dangerous for addicts, providing excuses where accountability and responsibility are desperately needed.

The last thing someone with an addiction problem needs is a free high. Those who are clinically depressed may need to be prescribed medication by a physician; there is nothing wrong with this practice. Certainly there are those who suffer from mental health disorders and addiction problems concurrently.

According to an article on "Ask Well" about alcohol and depression, Dr. Larissa Mooney, an associate clinical professor of psychiatry at U.C.L.A.'s Addiction Medicine Clinic stated: "Treatment for those addicted who show signs of depression is talk therapy, social support, and a combination of medications." Today the thinking is that depression and addiction should be treated at the same time. Unfortunately, Dr. Mooney doesn't comment on why some clinicians think depression and addiction should be treated at the same time.

I have talked with several doctors, mental health professionals, addiction professionals, and individuals from the recovery community, and the thinking is mixed on when someone should seek therapy or professional mental health guidance when suffering from addiction and signs of depression. It would be a shame for someone struggling to overcome addiction to be misdiagnosed and medicated for the wrong reason, and it would also be terrible for someone who truly needs medication for clinical depression to be denied the proper treatment and medication needed to find balance in their life.

It seems clear that everyone has their opinion on this complex and serious issue. If a diagnosis to medicate is nothing more than a guess, or someone is manipulating and seeking medication, unbeknownst to the doctor, and then there is a major problem with the system. *The DSM or Diagnostic and Statistical Manual of Mental Disorders* states that approximately one out of every two-hundred people in the United States may suffer from bipolar disorder. Compare that number to the number of people diagnosed as bipolar who suffer from addiction in the United States who have gone through treatment.

I doubt the numbers will be anywhere near the DSM assessment; too many people in early recovery are labeled with mental health disorders who may have no symptoms over time.

Do we have the cart before the horse, you decide for yourself. Occam's Razor may help!

Chapter Eight
Twelve Tips to Stay Sober Through the Holidays

Most individuals who suffer from or have had an issue with substance abuse or alcoholism in their lives know that the Holiday season is a tough time of year to get through. The seven-week period from before Thanksgiving to just after New Year's Day of holiday festivities, family gatherings, and parties can wreak havoc on sobriety and spirituality. These tips can help any time of year.

> *"What's the harm if you have just one?"* –
> *Holiday-Party Goer*

It seems like the mental obsession goes into overdrive for some people; is it euphoria, friends, and family enticing substance abusers to relapse without thinking, or maybe just the wanting to feel normal mentality that kick-start the emotions this time of year. Perhaps it's more of a desire to numb out the pain, than a desire to feel the pleasure that leads to such a high-risk to indulge in the reaper's games at this time of year.

The following twelve days through the holidays are tips that will help any substance abuser or alcoholic in recovery to stay in recovery during the holidays. Let's be honest if you were able to get clean and sober, then you have already made it through the hardest part of recovery. Now it's all about continued growth and maintenance.

Be prepared before you can execute anything. You need an action plan that sets you up for success. Action plans start with a goal, they are very specific with timetables and follow-up.

Who is going to do what, when are they going to do it, how are they going to do it, with who, and why are they going to do it?

Where are they going to do it, and who will they report the results to?

A good example would be, goal: go to office party without using. Plan: hire a recovery coach to accompany me to party. Complete this week, follow-up with a sponsor. Have recovery coach, order club soda with olives and stirrer for me at the party so that I won't hear, "Do you want a drink?" Follow-up with Coach at the party. Write out action plan before going to party, pros and cons list to see if it's worth going. Complete two weeks before the party, follow-up with a sponsor.

Increase your support network during the holidays. If you go to recovery meetings, go to more meetings during this period. If you have a recovery coach, schedule more sessions during this time. If you see a recovery counselor, schedule an extra session during this time. Use the telephone and communicate with other clean and sober friends. Learn to tell on yourself. If you feel like you're close to relapse, get honest with someone else.

"Christmas is not a date on a calendar. It's more than a state of mind. It's a condition of the heart."
– Toni Sorenson

Schedule a recovery retreat for yourself during the holidays. There are many recovery programs that offer "rest retreats" for those that have at least ninety days clean and sober. Give yourself the gift of sanity during the holidays, you deserve it! These retreats are great to get centered or work on a particular area of your life that needs work.

Travel during the holidays; however, take a clean and sober friend with you. It's a great time to get deals at resorts, on cruises, and other fun and exciting excursions. When's the last time that you treated yourself to something good? You can travel and still go to support meetings. If you can't find a meeting, have one with your traveling companion. Imagine, using your

Christmas club savings on a recovery vacation! Great clean and sober fun!

If any party or event places your recovery in harm's way, simply don't attend. Your life is more important than a holiday party. Think of a few excuses why you can't attend certain risky activities that would be acceptable to the host. "I'm sorry Jane, I won't be attending the party on Saturday, I'm having a minor surgery on Friday and will be laid up for a few days, recovering" "I'm sorry Bob, I'm going to be out of town on the 23rd; however, I'm sending a gift, and I am grateful for the invitation. I apologize that I can't be there to join you in person, but will be with you in spirit, have a wonderful party."

Remember the rules: stay away from slippery people, places, and things, especially around the holidays. Our senses seem to be intensified one hundred fold during the holiday season, make sure that you're not with those that are not good for your recovery. Alcoholics in recovery don't belong sitting in bars and night clubs; heroin addicts don't go to Christmas parties at their former dealer's house. We must be honest with ourselves here.

Remember that bars serve salty snacks for free for a reason, they make you want to consume more drinks! Avoid the salty snacks at parties as they will make you thirsty. If you must indulge, make sure that you have an alcohol-free beverage in hand already.

If you are a spiritual person, remember to utilize your spiritual tools of recovery to get through the holiday season. You may have favorite readings, meditations, prayers, a special place to go, meetings, people, a Higher Power, recovery activities, writing poetry, journaling, etc. These will bring you a great deal of strength during a difficult time and empower your sobriety.

Build a wall of sober defense around you, using loved ones, your support network, supportive friends, and family.

Make sure that your "people wall" is built of those that are supportive of your recovery and not those who would entice you to have "just one!" Make sure that you plan your support people ahead of time.

Communicate with your recovery coach, sponsor, counselor, therapist, or other recovery professionals about the emotions, expectations, and feelings about the complexity of the holiday season and your recovery and life. We all have that little boy or girl who lives inside us that as adults, we must nurture. "Sometimes, it is time to put childish things away!" Our expectations of the holidays need to be realistic, not a screaming child in Wonderland, "I want, I want, I want!" We all need to set reachable, realistic expectations on ourselves and others, all year round. We need to let go of old thinking and old ideas that made us sick and got us drunk and high. We need to remember to forgive and to do our best to do the next right thing, each and every day. We need to lose any sense of entitlement that we may still have, beware of rationalizations, and realize how vulnerable we actually can be around the holidays. Remember, addiction is "cunning, baffling powerful, and insidious!"

Focus on service work. "Move a muscle and change a thought!" The holidays are all about spirituality; it's a great time to focus on giving back and helping those less fortunate. Homeless shelters, soup kitchens, toys for tots, ministries, scholarship programs, non-profits, there are all kinds of opportunities to volunteer and help others. Service is a great way to get through the holidays and give back.

"The spirit of Christmas is found when we lift the load of others." – Toni Sorenson

---

Don't place yourself in harm's way. If you know that Bobby always has booze and drugs at his parties, don't go! If your sister Kate always calls you names because you're an addict and embarrasses you in front of friends and family, avoid her. Never put your recovery and life at risk for anyone, it's not worth it. You are more valuable than that!

Holidays or not, some individuals need treatment this time of year; in fact, many people start the recovery process between Thanksgiving and New Year's Day. Sobriety could be the best holiday gift that you and your loved ones ever received! In recovery, every day is a holiday because of attitude, and gratitude.

Chapter Nine
AMA/ APA: Leaving Against Medical or Professional Advice

AMA/APA: has been defined regarding any client or patient who insists upon leaving against the expressed advice of the treating team, Doctor, counselor, or other Professional. Not following the treatment plan, leaving detox prematurely, leaving residential treatment programs prematurely, not following through with therapist appointments, counseling appointments, etc.

Who is at risk of AMA/APA? Research has targeted admissions for alcohol, drug abuse, and psychiatric problems, Males, the poor. The truth is it could be anyone who gets caught up in the mental obsession of the disease of addiction!

If you are fortunate enough to get your loved one to go to treatment, through an interventionist, or because they were willing, consider your family as blessed! Most addicts never make it into treatment. Once they get into treatment, remember that they are scared, and at some point they will probably want to use their drug of choice again.

Expect your loved one to call home and complain about the treatment center: "Their mean to me here!" "The food is no good!" "There is no counseling here!" "There are people getting high here!" Your loved one will say anything they can to push your buttons! They know how to get to you so that you will come get them! Don't fall for it! Your loved one wants to use drugs! Let the professionals do their jobs.

Please trust the professionals that to help your loved one to recover from this deadly disease.

They are committed to helping your family. They need that same level of commitment from you to be strong and not enable your loved one. Together we can win this fight! Together we can save this life! Unity is key.

Case Study: Billy's Story
Billy somehow was able to get illicit drugs into another treatment facility and was caught during a random drug screening. Billy was asked to leave the facility. Bill's father called another facility and was able to get a bed for Billy the same day. The new facility took all the proper measures and Billy was admitted. Two days later Billy's father called the facility and asked for Billy's case Manager. Alice was Billy's case manager; she was summoned to the phone. The father stated that Billy had called him complaining about the food, the meetings, and that his room was dirty. Alice assured the father that everything was in order and that Billy just wanted to get high. They talked a few more minutes and ended the call. Two days later Alice was surprised to see Billy and his father exiting the building. The father stopped to talk to Alice for a moment and told Alice that Billy had called him again and said that the staff wasn't giving him anything to drink and that he was dehydrated. The father made the decision to take Billy home.

On the car ride home, Billy and the father had an argument. Billy got out of the vehicle and went to his girlfriend's house. He died from an overdose that night. The power of manipulation and enabling!

What could have and should have been done differently if anything?

Billy's father loved him to death! Don't let this be you!

Misconceptions by Families:
They think:
The loved one will be cured.
The loved one will return to an earlier time period when they were 'not an abuser'.

The loved one can maintain sobriety but still have 'just one drink.'
The loved one will not have any bad habits since they are sober.
Unresolved family issues will simply disappear.
The Family Unit has no issues independent of the substance abuser.
The Family Unit will return to a different more cohesive time period.
The substance abuser will not lie or manipulate anymore.
The substance abuser will not use again nor want to use again.
The substance abuser will leave treatment, find a job, and reintegrate into society as 'expected".

Case Management
Client orientation to treatment
Clarify expectations of provider
Link to outside world (resolve concerns)
Orient treatment provider
Monitoring client progress
Adjusting services plan as needed
Share client information when necessary (Respecting HIPAA regulations)
Drug testing
Structure boundaries
Advocacy needs may be revealed (discrimination, treatment refusal, etc.)
Meet short and medium term needs
Motivate and encourage
Set client up for success
Provide support
Intervene and respond to crisis
Promote independence
Develop external support to remove blockages
Clarify consequences
Clients have different paces
Encourage progress and positive outcomes
Planning, goal-setting, and implementation:
Distinct, manageable Goals and objectives
Time frames for completing

Celebrate successful completion of an objective
Failure to complete opportunity to re-evaluate one's efforts
Begin an advocacy process

Aftercare: (Long-Term Aftercare = Long-Term Recovery)
Case Manager coordinates all aspects of treatment
Drug-free home environment
Safe home
Medical and dental care
Pain management and medication (coordination and advocacy)
Identify personal relapse triggers
Intervene appropriately
Avoid slippery people, places, and things
Help client to master basic skill sets
Function independent in community
Short term goals: parenting, housekeeping, budgeting, etc.
Long term goals: recovery lifestyle
Sober Housing, ½ way and ¾ housing
Periodic outpatient
Recovery coaching (Professional or Peer)
Relapse prevention
Recovery groups, twelve-steps, and self-help groups
Counseling/therapy
Employment
Vocational Rehabilitation
Safe housing
Family coaching/counseling, support groups
Social services as needed
Case management communication

Keeping a client in a program, following the treatment plan of action successfully starts with the very first phone call. These are key factors that will help keep the client in treatment through the entire plan:

   1. Educating the family and or significant other.
   2. Clarifying Expectations.
   3. Having Releases signed so that you can communicate with family members and significant

other.
4. Building Trust with the client and the Family.
5. Having the family work as a team. Everyone must be on the same page.
6. Strong communication.
7. Proper Detoxification.
8. Educating and training facility staff.
9. Recovery & Education for the family too.
10. Taking away all the excuses and the getaway cars up front.
11. Support recovery, don't enable!
12. Relapse Prevention Groups.

So, what does all this mean? Pay Close Attention; this is important. This is where it all comes together and will start to make sense.

The best way to explain things is to take you through a case, step by step:

It all starts with the initial phone contact. Educating the family about what to expect starts right there. If the call is from the addicted person, you start to clarify expectations, build trust, and minimize fear.

If you tell the family what to expect in the first few weeks and teach them how to deal with their addicted loved one, there won't be any confusion, and they will trust you as the expert.

The staff also must be trained on how to handle the addicted person on the intake to minimize the potential for future problems. This is accomplished through education, training, and communication.

The extended family and friends must also be educated and trained by the core family unit to take away the "Get Away Car!" extra funds to the addicted family member, a place to stay, and any other enabling.

Once the addicted person is in your care, you must get releases signed so that you can continue to talk to the core family members. This is very important. You don't want to violate the HIPAA Regulations.

The family doesn't have to worry about HIPAA, only treating Professionals.

The more leverage the core family has, the better. Are they supporting their loved one? Does their loved one live with them? Are they paying for their loved one's lawyer? etc.

Know the history of the addicted person. Are they a Runner? What is their "Track" Record?

What resources does the core family have to work with? Do they have any family friends on the local Police Department? In the Judicial/ Court System or Local Government? Do they have a Lawyer in the Family? Is there a Doctor in the family? Who in the family can help the situation?

Educate the core family about enabling and Tough Love.

The family must make it clear to the addicted person that you're there for them and stress how important commitment is in recovery and life.

Case study:
~Johnny is a Heroin Addict.

~Parents called for help; they are married Sue & Sam Doe.

~Johnny lives with the parents; he is eighteen years old.

~He has been to two treatment centers and has left both programs after less than ten days.

~He has a girlfriend Hanna that is everything! Hanna has a car.

~There is a lawyer in the family, Sam's brother.

~Sue and Hanna are enablers.

~The initial screening call is complete.

~Johnny has agreed with parents to go to treatment.

~Johnny is High Risk for AMA!

~What do you do next?

~All four people show up for intake at 10 AM Monday morning.

~Prior to intake, the parents should have been educated about the intake process. The facility could have picked Johnny up. Being that the two women are enablers, the father should have driven John alone. Then there would be no pressure on John.

~The father asks on intake, "Can I just pay for two weeks, instead of the whole month?" I'm sorry sir, but no! We teach addicted people the importance of commitment. The message Johnny would get is that you are not committed, so why should he be. If you were to pay for two weeks in John's mind, he would be geared up to leave in fourteen days. Our policy is a min. of thirty days paid on intake or before.

~While the staff searches through John's luggage, the secretary offers Sam a cup of coffee. (Stop! Another Mistake!)

~As soon as any financial paperwork is taken care of and the first month is paid for, all family and friends should leave and let John get settled in. This way, he can't get cold feet and panic and want to leave. The "Get Away Car" is gone!

~Have someone who is a positive member of the group shadow Johnny to make him feel welcome and a part of. Make sure staff does a complete search for contraband coming in such as drugs other items that are not allowed into the facility.

Send John's cell phone home with Sam, so he can't call a "Get Away Car!" Some facilities have a blackout period for payphone use. In this case, it would be two weeks because John is a runner.

~Should John break the rules and call home the core family should already have been instructed what to say and do. The first thing is to say, are you allowed to call us right now? If not, hang up! If they do talk with John, only positive things about his recovery. Nothing about: home or girlfriend. No enabling. No listening to complaining or wanting to leave. Limit calls to one a week.

~The core family needs to get extended family and friends on board about not taking calls or picking John up if he wants to leave treatment. The toughest one will be the girlfriend. Perhaps the core family and the uncle that is the lawyer could invite her to the house for a meeting and explain the gravity of the situation. If she picks him up from treatment, perhaps the family lawyer will have something to say to her about responsibility if he should die.

~Continue to educate that no one should send John any form of money, pick him up, send transportation, or provide quarters.

~While he is in treatment, the core family needs to search the house and vehicles for drugs and related items and get rid of them. A family Recovery Coach would be great to assist with all of this! No visitors for John for at least three weeks.

~What if John says, "I need shampoo!" Send him the shampoo, not money! Support recovery, but do not Enable Addiction!

~The staff at the facility should be trained in how to handle John should he be going through emotions and want to leave anyway. The staff should be able to read his body language, tones, and inflections. The staff should be able to engage in powerful questioning and active listening, sharing their experience, strength, and hope to turn John around.

The key is to get John to stay in the day, one day at a time. It's also key for John to see the truth and not buy the lie of the disease of addiction any longer.

~All new guests should have a roommate that is positive that is not new!

~All new guests should attend a relapse prevention meeting in their first few days at the facility.

Let's take a look at what has been accomplished:

1. John is educated, and we have clarified expectations for him.
2. The core family and The Extended Family and Friends are educated and trained on what to do and not do.
3. We have taken away all of the excuses and the "Get Away Cars!"
4. John has no funds to leave.
5. John has no cell phone.
6. John has nowhere to stay.
7. The staff is educated and trained on what to do and what not to do.
8. The enablers are out of the picture.
9. John has attended relapse prevention group.
10. John has a positive and experienced roommate.
11. The core family hired a family recovery coach to aid them through.
12. The house is free from drugs and related items.
13. No Visitors for John for at least three weeks.

The chances of John being an AMA are very slim compared to his past couple of times in treatment. He could still try to run. This is not a perfect science. The idea is that we want to do everything we can to reduce the odds that a client becomes an AMA. Sometimes they just panic because they want drugs and there isn't anything that can stop them!

Now Johnny and the family are set up for success!

Chapter Ten
Grandparents: The Unsung Heroes of Addiction Epidemic

Many grandparents are raising their grandchildren because of addiction! Perhaps their son or daughter was lost to an overdose or their still in active addiction. Responsibility and accountability demonstrate the willingness necessary to recover from addiction; for many suffering from addiction raising their own children in the early recovery process is just too much for them.

You can't give away what you don't have. In some cases, where a young person suffering from addiction is trying to bring up a child, it's like a toddler trying to raise an infant. It seems as if whatever age the drug abuser started using drugs and alcohol, they stopped growing inter-personally, spiritually, and emotionally. A twenty-two-year-old that began using as a young teen in many ways is still like a young teenager. How could they ever raise a child; many still need parenting themselves.

Many of the pregnancies that happen under the influence are unplanned and unwanted. Some of the females are sexually assaulted while under the influence, and either don't believe in abortion or can't afford one. Scores of males are irresponsible when drunk or high and are not ready to settle down and raise a child at such a young age. The situation can become a terrible burden for elderly grandparents both physically and financially.

I often wonder how many people got trapped in the lives they are presently living because of extenuating circumstances, such as illness of a loved one getting into a relationship at a young age, having a child at a young age, an unexpected disability, a divorce, or other unforeseen events? I'm sure that there are many people who function like robots, going to work day after day, week after week in a job that they aren't happy with. Numerous people get trapped in a relationship that they're not happy with as well; some make great sacrifices to benefit others.

Imagine spending your lifetime taking care of an ill sibling, parent, child, or grandchild. Or raising someone else's children because they were not able to, or taking in an elderly person who has no family and helping them daily. These can be lifelong commitments. It takes a very particular kind of person to do this; these people are real heroes! They give up their dreams and their futures to help others. They are real servants.

In my family, I witnessed my mother and father raise three granddaughters because of their father's addictions and the turmoil it leads to in the children's home. My mom and dad were already in their late fifties, and they spent another two decades raising children. Stress, burden, and unfair expectations were placed on my elderly parents. They did what they needed to do for the family out of love. They should have received an award for all the chaos they lived through with those three girls! My parents were amazing people. It does take special people to make such sacrifices.

Every few minutes another person suffering from addiction losses the battle against addiction, and their life, leaving behind orphaned or single-parented children. Those that use dirty needles and get infected with AIDS can also lose their lives. Thousands and thousands of people have died; someone has to care for their children after they're gone.

The unsung heroes in the war against addiction are the children and the grandparents. Last Thursday I received a call from a close friend in New Jersey, the message brought the reaper. Our friend Jason had overdosed, leaving behind two young sons. Jason was a young man himself, too young to die! I wept for his sons; they're only little boys. Who will care for them and support them now? I would imagine the grandparents will step in and help out.

Some people take very low paying jobs that help others, such as social workers, counselors, case managers, etc.
These people work very hard, work long hours, and get very little financial reward. This too is a special breed of people.

They are beautiful, committed, caring individuals.

Where would all the poor souls that need help and assistance every day be without all these wonderful and faithful people? Their quality of life wouldn't even be close to what it is today. To all of you that help the less fortunate, who stand in the gap week after week, month after month, and year after year Thank you! You are truly heroes! God bless you for all that you do!

Chapter Eleven
Signs of Drug Use & Keys to Family Recovery

Are there drugs hidden in your house?

You may stop and think that you should not snoop on your kids, but remember, it's your house! What would you say to the police if they showed up at your house and said that drugs were being sold from your house?

Good places to look:
    Dresser drawers, beneath or between clothes
    Desk drawers also taped behind or above.
    CD/DVD/Tape/Video cases
    Small boxes – jewelry, pencil, etc.
    Backpacks/duffel bags
    Under a bed: look for holes in the mattress.
    In a plant, buried in the dirt
    Between books on a bookshelf
    In books with pages cut out
    Makeup cases – inside fake lipstick tubes or compacts
    Under a loose plank in floor boards
    In fake soda bottles with false bottoms
    Inside over–the–counter medicine containers (Tylenol, Advil, etc.)
    Inside empty candy bags or containers.
    Up in ceiling tiles.
    In toilet tanks.
    Shoes and sneakers under inserts.
    Coffee cans, cereal boxes

        Behaviors to look for when using:
           a. Change in relationships at home and friends
           b. Loss of inhibitions
           c. Mood changes, drastic swings
           d. Loud and obnoxious behavior
           e. Laughing for no reason
           f. Unusually clumsy, off-balance

    g. Withdrawn, depressed
    h. More tired than usual
    i. Not communicating, silent
    j. Hostile, Secretive, Full of excuses
    k. Talking rapid fire or slowly, slurred speech
    l. Lethargic, abnormal sleep patterns, can't focus

Look for use and abuse before your addicted loved one slips in a relapse and learn to recognize full-blown use.

  Personal Appearance when using drugs:
    a. Messy, Careless appearance
    b. Poor Hygiene
    c. Track Marks on arms or legs
    d. Burns or soot on fingers, lips
    e. Red flushed face
    f. Bloodshot eyes/pinned pupils
    g. Scratch marks or pimples on face, neck, arms, back

Look for Physical as Well as Emotional Signs of Use.

  Personal Habit Changes:
    a. The smell of smoke on breath or clothes (could be from others)
    b. Now chewing gum and mints around you
    c. Using eye drops
    d. Breaking curfew
    e. Cash Flow problems
    f. Avoids eye contact
    g. Clenches teeth
    h. Going out every night
    i. Secretive calls, texts, friends, etc.
    j. Major Munchies all of the sudden
    k. The use of air fresheners, incense, scented candles, perfumes, and colognes.
    l. Prescriptions disappearing
    m. Missing alcohol and cigarettes
    n. Valuables and money disappearing
    o. Unusual smell in the car

    p. Bottles, pipes, bongs, foil, lighters in the car
    q. Unusual containers, wrappers, seeds
    r. Be aware of soda cans, shaving cream cans, etc. that the tops or bottoms screw off as stash boxes for drugs.
    s. Aluminum Foil with abstract black lines
    t. Rolled up Dollar bills
    u. Little plastic bags, or little bottles
    v. White powder residue

What Changes When Your Loved One Is Using and What to Look for but Not Over Obsess About. Just to Be Aware.

    Health Issues:
        a. Nosebleeds
        b. Runny Nose
        c. Frequently sick
        d. Sores around mouth
        e. Nauseous
        f. Seizures
        g. Vomiting
        h. Cotton Mouth
        i. Drastic weight loss or gain
        j. Skin abrasions, bruises
        k. Depression
        l. Headache
        m. Sweatiness

Health Issues and Signs of Use

    School and Work Related:
        a. Loss of interest
        b. Grades are dropping
        c. Reports of intoxication
        d. No interest in extracurricular activities
        e. Failure to fulfill responsibilities

Keys to Family Recovery:

1. Importance of Self-Care
   a. Family members and people pleasers will forget about their own needs.
   b. New problems arise and the family is neglected.
   c. Day to day affairs of the family not taken care of properly.
   d. The main supporter gets overwhelmed and sometimes sick.

2. Set Healthy Boundaries.
   a. Limit personal space.
   b. Don't accept blame of others.
   c. There must be consequences.
   d. Keep your promises.
   e. Do not make promises or bribes for the abuser to recover.

3. Learning to validate your words.
   a. No means. No.
   b. Take your needs out of the picture. Not about you.
   c. Focus.
   d. If your abuser needs shampoo, buy shampoo. Don't give cash.

4. Accusations are not the truth.
   a. Addicts' instinct is to lie.
   b. Remember, it's not about you.
   c. Substance abusers do not like confrontation; they will manipulate and be dishonest.
   d. Substance abusers will twist the facts to people please.
   e. Substance abusers will tell you what you want to hear to get what they want.
   f. Addicts will tell you they completed tasks that they want to complete or plan to complete. (aka the garbage is taken out but it is still sitting in the trash can)

5. Should you use drug tests?
    a. The mistake families make is to drug test frequently. It will put the client on edge, and they will use more often.
    b. Use a recovery coach or outpatient to drug test.
    c. Drug test without questioning.

6. Building trust back takes time.
    a. You have to let go of resentments.
    b. Learn to trust based on behavior.
    c. Identifying hidden blame and resentment
    d. Do trust-building activities with the family.

Chapter Twelve
Suicides & Overdoses are Reality

Mothers and fathers are not supposed to bury their children. What happened to all of the dreams and hopes; where did they all go?

Another time back, crimson mixed with poison pierces young flesh and a soul nods forever. One by one, friends and family are lost.

Then the horror show begins as mother's shriek and fathers cry. Loved ones, broken-hearted, pace the floor - night after night, like a tormented ghost. The pain is unbearable for everyone that loved you. You killed a part of everyone, altered futures, dreams, and lives. Nothing will ever be the same.

Did you think any of this through before you plunged the spike into your arm? Fun you thought, entertainment, killing pain? Take a look at all the suffering in the world because of drugs and addiction; where exactly is the fun, entertainment, and any value at all?

I wish you could see what's happening now, because if you could, this never would have happened. I know that no son, daughter, sister, brother, or friend could ever want to cause this much grief.

> **What was causing you so much pain?**
> **Why didn't you share it with any of us?**
> **Why couldn't you trust us with your pain?**
> **Did we ever tell you how valuable you were?**
> **Did you even know how much we all loved you?**

My God, maybe we didn't deserve your trust! Maybe we were all too busy to hear and see that you needed a friend, someone to talk to, and someone to care. Possibly all you ever needed was a friend, not a needle.

Maybe all you needed was someone to show you unconditional love.

I think the needle and the drugs are just a symptom of the problem that's killing our kids and our friends. Addiction is a thinking and a living problem, not a drug problem. Maybe all that is needed is love, understanding, time, and caring for those that need it.

I wish we had all done a better job being there for you in your life so that you didn't feel like you needed to use drugs. I wish we could have shown you how valuable you were, and how much you meant to us. Maybe we didn't show you how to live in this world without drugs.

Admittedly this is a hard world to live in for young people, it must be very scary:

- **It costs a fortune to get a college education**
- **There aren't any jobs after you graduate college**
- **Terrorist activity and war are common occurrences**
- **The daily news is enough to scare and discourage anyone**
- **Most of the population are struggling financially**

I understand that your life is hard, but drugs are not, have not, and will never be the answer. Death is forever! You don't have to die from a drug overdose; it's a choice! Remember that it will do all the things that I said it will do; I've witnessed them all too many times to remember.

When addiction claims another life, it takes everyone involved - and their family and friends don't have a choice, they are hostage to the emotions, regrets, and guilt.
Family and friends forever wonder if they did something wrong. It's a horrible reality that people have to exist in; I say exist because life is over at that point.

> *Get Help "What kills a person at twenty-five? Leukemia. An accident. But George knows the better odds are that someone who passes at that age dies of unhappiness. Drug overdose. Suicide. Reckless behavior."* — Scott Turow

And it doesn't have to be this way.

If you have an addiction problem, think it through, it's not just about you. The overdose is coming; it will happen. Kids are dying every few minutes from drug overdoses.

Soon you too will nod the nod of forever. Lives, futures, and dreams all ruined!

It's happening in every town, in every state of this country and all over the World. It's an epidemic!

But you can make a difference today!

Talk to your friends and your children; help them understand that awareness, education, and prevention work.

If you're an addict, get help! You don't have to die, and you're not alone. Don't be another statistic, a number, a toe tag!

Be alive and dream dreams, live your life, set goals and surpass them! Spread the love, the hope, and the message that no one has to die! Choose life!

When I was a young man growing up in the '70s and '80s, it was rare to hear of anyone dying from drugs or alcohol. Every once in a while you would see on the news that a famous musician or movie star had overdosed; from time to time, you would hear about a fatal car crash involving drugs and alcohol. Kids never died from drugs or alcohol in school, it just didn't happen; there was one exception, suicide!

Shame is the core of addiction and self-centeredness is at the root. When a person becomes addicted to a substance, their spirit becomes blocked by harmful self or self-centeredness. Because the spirit is blocked the person doesn't grow emotionally and spiritually as they should; the basic instincts become out of balance, social, security, sexual and in come fears, resentments, and harms.

Shame is a killer just as powerful as an addiction; make no mistake about it! The isms of addiction can be present in a young person before they even experience the use of drugs or alcohol, or their first high. A young person may not be happy with the way they look, their intelligence, their family, their social class, their home, sexuality, or religion. Or they may be dealing with other issues such as abuse, broken homes, adoption, abandonment or bullying by other students or siblings. They may not have any coping skills to deal with the enormous pressures that young people face as they go through life, and no mentors or role models. Drugs today are everywhere; peer pressures are enormous! It almost seems natural to these kids to reach for something to kill their pain, to numb out the world. When the pain becomes unbearable, suicide becomes a realistic option for them.

Teen suicide is an escalating health concern and one of the leading causes of death for young people ages fifteen to twenty-four, according to the United States Center for Disease Control and Prevention. Suicidal risk factors do vary according to stress, family unit and dynamics, age, ethnic background, gender, and sexuality. Mental illness is the leading risk factor for suicide; however, psychological, social, and environmental factors can cause suicidal thoughts and actions.

I also want to mention that Pathological Gambling is three to four times more likely to affect teenagers than older people. Problem Gambling is the number one addiction related to suicide. One in five Pathological Gamblers will attempt suicide.

In 2004, The National Institute of Mental Health distributed a report showing research with the main risk factors for suicide. More than ninety percent of people who die by suicide have three risk factors: mental health disorders, depression, and substance abuse. Stressors for teens are interpersonal losses, being victims of bullying, domestic violence, confusion and shame about sexual orientation, abuse, and disciplinary issues. Possible warning signs to watch for suicidal ideation:

Low self-esteem
Sleep pattern changes (insomnia)
Eating habits change (not eating or overeating)
Mood swings (down, apathetic, withdrawn, anxiety, irritable)
Behavior changes (lack of concentration, not caring)
No hope (no hope for change)
Any recent loss (death or break up)
Constantly focusing and talking about death and dying
Self-harm
Acting erratically

According to data collected by the CDC back in 2003, twenty percent of all teenagers in the United States seriously consider suicide annually; eight percent attempt suicide, which represents approximately one million teens; 300,000 received medical attention, and approximately 1,700 teens die by suicide each year.

Today there are community-based teen screening programs in place, school-based suicide prevention programs, and a national suicide prevention Lifeline: 1-800-273-TALK. Awareness, education, and prevention are the answer to help solve this terrible problem.

At present, our nation is in the middle of an epidemic that is killing our kids! It's not that they are necessarily suicidal; it's that when they do decide to reach for a drug to numb out the pain for the first time, it can be fatal.

Opiate use is happening in every town, in every state in the country. Our kids and adults are dying every few minutes from opiate use.

We know that genetics, utero and early childhood traumas and stress can impact a human being in many ways: addiction, brain circuitry, mental health issues, physical issues, etc. I believe there are a great deal of similarities with teenagers and famous people here: both groups don't know who they are and feel tremendous pressure from the world around them. Usually, both groups are loved by many people; however, they feel lonely even in crowds. They put unrealistic expectations on themselves and are their worst critics. The one they need to please is themselves.

Every problem has a solution, as the problem defines the solution. There are perception and perspective problems that block the solution at times. But certainly drugs and alcohol never were and never will be the answer to any problem. Nor is suicide ever the answer. No matter what the problem is, there is help, and there are people who care.

There is too much pain in this world, but there is a mountain of love if you know where to look for it! Sometimes we try too hard, we go too fast, we do too much and we miss the simple pleasures in life, like living itself, breathing, sunlight, spending the day with your dog, your family, having one good friend, enjoying a good book, sitting out at night looking up at the stars, and so many other precious gifts that surround us. We should never take these things for granted.

If you or someone you know needs help, please know that there is help available and that no one has to die from mental illness or addiction. Call the helplines today. If no one else told you today that they love you, it doesn't mean they don't; somewhere in this world someone is thinking good thoughts about you right this minute! You matter, you have a purpose and a place, and a right to be! Best of life friends!

In the '80s, I was a young police officer and a high school athletic coach. In the fall, one night during wrestling season I had an experience that would change my life and worldview forever. That fateful night would change numerous perspectives, perceptions and lives both young and old.

The day started out like any other: I worked the 11 PM to 7 AM shift at the department, slept for seven hours, went to a three-hour wrestling practice, showered and ate then back to work. I always made sure my uniform was ready, shoes shined, badge polished, everything perfect.

I went to work about thirty minutes early as usual. I joined the rest of my shift in the roll-call room and waited for the sergeant. Depending on how many officers were on shift, we would be assigned to different sections of the town for the shift. There is always a shift supervisor, a sergeant, and five to ten officers.
The sergeant is assigned to the desk to answer the calls and log them; the sergeant also sends officers to answer calls. I was assigned to the north end of town that night.

Friday nights on the graveyard shift could be extremely quiet or very hectic; it was always a roll of the dice! There were a couple of minor motor-vehicle accidents earlier on the shift. A couple of the officers were running radar on one of the main roads in town. I was patrolling the north end of town; there wasn't much happening early in the shift. Then I heard the sergeant's voice come over the radio; he was calling me in unit or car number six. He called out a code that I never had heard anyone call before and an address; I could tell by the tones and inflections of his voice that it was something bad!

I turned on the strobe lights and siren and drove as fast as possible to the address the sergeant had called out. When I turned down the street the house was on; a young man waved me down at the end of the driveway. I drove down the driveway, and there were hysterical teenagers wandering all over the property. They were all visibly shaken, crying and in shock! I still wasn't sure what was going on?

When I got to the end of the driveway some of the kids that I coached came up to me, they grabbed me by the hand and took me into the house to show me what had happened. They were so shaken that they couldn't even talk!

What I witnessed next was one of the most horrible incidents that I have ever seen in my life! I will not describe the gruesome details of what I will never forget to you; however, I will explain an overview. A sixteen-year-old young man's stepfather and mother went away on a trip. He asked if he could have his friends over while the parents were gone and was denied. The young man invited all his friends from school over for a party and blender drinks, they were all having fun and partying, not knowing he was in distress. The young man took his stepfather's 30-30 rifle into the parent's master bedroom and committed suicide.

All the young man's friends were there and witnessed this terrible scene! We were all traumatized! There is no training that can prepare you for a situation like I witnessed that dreadful night! When I finished my shift, I went home and finished a bottle of Irish whiskey as well.

The kids from my teams insisted that I take them to the viewing a few days later. The truth is, I didn't want to go at all, and I knew it would be very painful. Sure enough, when the deceased young man's mother's eyes locked on mine, and she grabbed my hand, it seemed like an eternity! It was like she was holding on to her son's life; it was painful, awkward, and very hard. I'm glad that the kids talked me into going; it was healing for everyone.

Seventeen years later I was attending a men's meeting at a residential facility on the East Coast. There were between twenty-five and thirty men ranging from late teens to mid-40s, most of the guys were very young. We were sitting in a circle in folding chairs outside in the sunshine. All of the sudden, most of the young men started talking about suicide; some were saying how they didn't care about their lives. I fought it until my hand shot up practically by itself!

The waterworks started flowing! I told the men the story that I had stuffed for all those years from that Friday night in the fall, and I shared my pain with them. I lost it, I couldn't stop crying, and I was so embarrassed. I was so enraged that I kicked my folding chair straight up into the air and went inside. I thought I had made a fool of myself!

I was in the men's room splashing some water on my face a few minutes later. I had left the group right before it was time for the group to end. Right, then the youngest member of our group came in the room and said, "I know you're embarrassed right now, but there's something you should know, it took a big man to do what you just did, and the guys couldn't even close the group because everybody was crying!" I believe that was a God moment.

I didn't realize that I had stuffed the pain all those years. I didn't even know that I was still in pain. Just by sharing honestly with others, it healed all of us, it was amazing. I hate seeing young people waste their lives. I see all the potential and promise that can be some day if they work hard.

Suicide is never the right answer! It ruins the lives of everyone that loves and cares about the person. For anyone who is thinking that they are hopeless and alone, know that you are not alone and that there is hope. Where there is life, there is always hope! Please call and get help today! Awareness, prevention, and education save lives!

National Suicide Prevention Lifeline 1-800-273-8255

References

(American Psychological Association, 2015) American psychological association. (2015). Teen suicide is preventable. Retrieved from http://www.apa.org/research/action/suicide.aspx ("Cyber Bullying leads to teen suicide") ("Teen Suicide Statistics") Cyber Bullying leads to teen suicide. (2007, November 17). Retrieved from http://abcnews.go.com/GMA/story?id=3882520amp;page=2Teen Suicide Statistics. Retrieved from teen suicide statistics website

Chapter Thirteen
The Importance of Commitment

A commitment is a promise or a model of change, a contract, or an involuntary commitment. All of these different definitions could have meaning to someone suffering from addiction and their family. Commitments are very important for substance abusers, no matter how small or big. I try to teach that to anyone that suffers from any form of addiction, and explain in detail why commitments must be kept to their family members. Accountability and responsibility demonstrate the willingness necessary to recover. In most cases those that are addicted have the best of intentions, and then the mental obsession and the phenomenon of craving take over. Those in active addiction never follow through with anything, with the exception of scoring drugs! Substance abusers lie, they cheat, and they steal when in the mental obsession of addiction. They will do anything to get high and to protect the supply. You can't count on someone suffering from addiction for anything else, you can't trust them; substance abusers can't even trust themselves. I'm not saying that they're bad people; I am saying that they're sick people. In recovery a substance abuser can't try the easier softer way, they can't use half measures. They won't get anywhere and won't have a positive result.

Substance abusers have to follow through and complete tasks on a timely basis. It's a whole new way of living, a better way. They will balk at first until it becomes a habit to keep commitments. When your loved one is in treatment, and the contract says sixty days, don't let them come home in thirty-seven. Make them, or help them to keep their commitment. If they sign a contract to go to a sober house for four months, don't let them come home in two months because you miss them. You're only enabling them in addictive behavior. Don't be a part of the problem, be a part of the solution. Substance abusers need to do what they say they are going to do. They need to mean what they say without saying it mean!

They need to keep and follow through with all commitments unless that commitment is still to illicit drugs and alcohol! If that's the case, they will need a different type of commitment! In some states, they have enacted statutes to assist law enforcement and families to force chronic addicts and those with severe mental health issues into treatment, such as the Baker and Marchman Acts in Florida and Connecticut. For those that are serious about recovery, they must follow through with a comprehensive action plan that will lead to an entire psychic change. This will not be easy because it will deviate from the norm in the majority of cases. Case managers, sponsors, recovery coaches, sober companions and family recovery coaches can be of great assistance in this area. The substance abuser's family also needs to follow through with a plan of action where they support recovery without enabling their addict. Please know there is hope and help for every substance abuser and alcoholic today. When the family shows that they're committed, it helps the substance abuser to be committed.

Chapter Fourteen
Parents Use Your Words Wisely

In my thirty-five years of dealing with the inner wounds of other people's sons and daughters, I have discovered the terrible and wonderful power of words in the lives of young people.

"...of all the weapons of destruction that man could invent, the most terrible-and the most powerful-was the word. Daggers and spears left traces of blood; arrows could be seen at a distance. Poisons were detected in the end and avoided. But the word managed to destroy without leaving clues." — *Paulo Coelho*

Words can be very powerful, even life changing or ending! What I thought I heard you say, isn't what you meant to say, or what you actually did say, because your thoughts and words were not the same as my understanding, and my perception of your words is much different than yours!

Wow is that a mouthful!

Often what we say, or think we say, or mean to say, is not what other people hear. Especially with our children, we have to be very careful with our words as parents.

For example, your daughter comes home from school, and you say to her, "Beth, I love you, but why can't you get good grades like your sister Alice does?"

You think that you told Beth that you love her and that she needs to improve her grades.

What Beth heard you say was, "Beth, your sister Alice is much better than you; you're not good at anything!"

You Said, What!

I hate texts from other people; they can be misinterpreted very easily. You can't read the other person's body language, tones, or inflections. Sometimes it's very hard to understand what another person meant.

The worst is when someone thinks that another person has made them a promise by the words that they said to them. The person now has high expectations of this perceived promise that is not even a reality.

Because of a miscommunication a friendship could be lost, a family dissolved, trust and faith in each other ruined. All because of lack of clarity in the spoken word; perhaps because one party did not listen carefully to what the other party had to say.

Listening is the most powerful communication skill that we have as human beings.

Those who master this skill will have a major advantage over other people in business, relationships, and in life. When we listen, we pick up on other subtle nuances in what is said because:

- **55% of communication is body language**
- **38% is tones and inflections**
- **7% is the spoken word**

Mastering the skills of reading body language, tones, and inflections will also give a person a huge advantage in life over other people.

These skills are all priceless in the business world, relationships, recovery and in general.

Verbal Abuse Hurts, Too

We all know that physical abuse hurts; a punch, kick, a pull of the hair! Verbal abuse can be just as painful, especially to children. At times, this happens, and the abuser is not even aware that they are abusive. Words can hurt people!

Think before you speak; there can be life ending consequences.

If you think about the first example of Beth and the message that she heard her parent say. She carried a lie in her spirit for years after that day.

The lie was that she was faulty, no good, didn't measure up, less than, a loser, not intelligent, and that her sister was loved more by the parents.

The only way for Beth to get better is for someone to tell her the truth and for Beth to let go of the old belief.

Beth needs a new directive; that she is a good person, that she has a purpose and a place, a right to be, and that she is a good person who is loved by her family.

The old directive must be taken away, and Beth must believe and buy into the new directive. This process most often involves self-discovery, prayer, and meditation.

Learning new directives is a process of real inner healing that takes place and changes the belief of the person.

Even single letters can end you up behind bars! If you ever get pulled over for suspicion of drunk driving, you better know your ABCs!

If you slur or mix up a few letters, chances are, you're going to spend the night in the drunk tank!

All because of a few letters; or maybe reality is because of a few too many drinks?

How about the power of the letters after some people's names with their credentials. Some have long lists of degrees and certifications that tell you how far they went in school and other special degrees and certifications. These letters can have a great deal of meaning and power when it comes to respect, employment, careers, education, and business.

For Christians, the Word means the Bible and the Word of God. These words are considered by many as the ultimate words of power! Some don't believe in these words at all, and others base their very lives on them. This decision is an individual choice based on culture, family, Worldview, and religion.

In today's world, we have texting, Twitter, Facebook, fax machines, cell phones, all kinds of social media, video games, Xbox, PlayStation, DIRECTV, Cable, Laptops, Kindles, tablets, desktops, Smartphones, GoToMeeting, YouTube, LinkedIn, Pinterest, Instagram, and Skype. However, what is lost is the art of face to face communication.

Utilizing the spoken word, reading body language, tones, and inflections, understanding active listening, is slowly becoming a lost art form.

The more people lose the understanding of human communication; the more chaos in the World will come. Communication brings consistency and teamwork that benefits every human being on the planet.

Perhaps the greatest form of words is lyrics! Music can pierce our very souls; cut through like a knife, touch us at our very core. Have you ever listened to the lyrics and the melody of a song that just hit you square in the heart and soul?

Everyone loves some form of music. Even the deaf can feel the rhythm of the beat. Music touches all us on a core level.

Music is the Universal language; so is love they say! Then of course poetry, prose, and books touch our lives; they educate, culture, and refine us. The words can help us dream dreams, visit places without moving, know characters we've never met, and learn things without a professor standing in front of us. We can share the hearts, minds, and spirits of others and ourselves through words.

There is such wonderful and great power in words.

I hope that you heard what I intended to say in this book. The only way that I will ever know is if you share a few words with me in the comment section. I hope you enjoy the power of words and that you use them wisely for the good of humanity and the World.

Chapter Fifteen
Important Terms & Definitions

Professional Recovery Coaching: It's about a results and client driven service that helps the client reach their goals and objectives by utilizing a variety of skills, tools, and techniques, and core competencies that assist in finding a solution. In many ways, recovery coaching is similar to sports coaching. Both services help the client to develop technical expertise, set performance targets, stay focused, cope with stresses, motivate the client, teach proper technique, chase out negativity, develop a vision, and celebrate the wins! Coaches are as much trainers of the mind as they are of the body.

Recovery Coach: -Recovery coaching is a form of strengths-based support for persons with addictions or in recovery from alcohol, other drugs, codependency, or other addictive behaviors. Recovery coaches work with persons with active addictions as well as persons already in recovery. Recovery coaches are helpful for making decisions about what to do with your life and the part your addiction or recovery plays. Recovery Coaches help clients find ways to stop addiction (abstinence), or reduce the harm associated with addictive behaviors. Recovery coaches can help a client find resources for harm reduction, detox, treatment, family support and education, local or online support groups; or help a client create a change plan to recover on their own.

Recovery coaches do not offer primary treatment for addiction, do not diagnose, and are not associated with any particular method or means of recovery. Recovery coaches support any positive change, helping persons coming home from treatment to avoid relapse, build community support for recovery, or work on life goals not related to addiction such as relationships, work, education, etc. Recovery coaching is action oriented with an emphasis on improving present life and reaching goals for the future.

Recovery coaching is unlike most therapy because coaches do not address the past, do not work to heal trauma, and there is little emphasis on feelings. Recovery coaches are unlike licensed addiction counselors in that coaches are non-clinical and do not diagnose or treat addiction or any mental health issues.

Telephone or Virtual Recovery Coach: A Telephone or Virtual Recovery Coaching relationship may be established to continue beyond the face to face meeting with a client and a recovery coach, sober escort or a sober companion coach. The prior face-to-face coaching relationship was built on trust and re-established honesty for the client, so the Telephone or Virtual Recovery Coach relationship can continue in the same light, with daily or weekly telephone or web-based conversations

Today, many treatment centers are embracing virtual recovery coaching and linking Telephone or Virtual Recovery Coaches to clients prior to leaving treatment as a way to continue the connection to the treatment center, as well as meeting guidelines of an 'aftercare' program. Online virtual coaching programs have also sprung up recently, either fee based or for free, that will help anyone apply the methods of recovery (e.g. developing a recovery plan and building recovery capital) whether the person has departed from a 30-day stay at a treatment center or relapsed many months after treatment.

Legal Support Specialist: Recovery Coach - Recently, lawyers dealing with criminal drug cases or drug courts have been requesting a type of recovery coaching to ensure a client, (perhaps under house arrest, enrolled in a drug court outpatient program or pending trial) stays sober as per the law's mandate. Recovery Coaches with the required certification and legal knowledge are contracted for this purpose. Coaches licensed as a Licensed Clinical Social Worker or Certified Alcohol and Drug Counselor with training in assessments can perform these tasks. The courts request them to perform a client assessment. The coach will then draft a letter to the court and offer suggested placement in a residential alcohol/drug treatment center, an outpatient treatment program and a sober living facility.

A Legal Support Specialist - Recovery Coach can also appear in court with the client and provide transportation to or from the courthouse.

History of Recovery Coaching: In 1984, the rock group Aerosmith was attempting a comeback, Joe Perry, and Steven Tyler, front men for the group, are referred to as the "Toxic Twins" for their heroin habits and other behaviors on and off the stage. In fact, the entire band was heavily drinking or taking drugs. While touring for the new album, the co-manager hired a psychiatrist to tour with the band. After a month, the doctor claimed the band was "unfixable." In order to survive they had to get sober. Some of the Band members became sober by the fall of 1986. Steven Tyler went to an in-treatment drug rehabilitation center, followed by Joe Perry. By the end of 1986, the final band member Brad Whitford had accepted sobriety. Heavy metal rockers on the road, with roadies, groupies, opening acts and exposure to more drugs and alcohol, in order to promote their newest album, Permanent Vacation. The manager was able to help the group, maintain sobriety throughout the tour by contacting a recovery coach, **Bob Timmons** to tour with the band. Recovery coaching had begun.

In 2003 Recovery Coaching became more developed and professional as a professional life-coaching niche. Alida Schuyler, a coach, credentialed by the International Coach Federation (ICF) wrote the first recovery coach certification training program.

Addiction recovery scholar and expert William L. White used the term "recovery coach" in his 2006 paper Sponsor, Recovery Coach, Addiction Counselor; however, later adopted the term "Peer Recovery Support Specialist" to emphasize a community-based peer model of addiction support. Recovery coaches use different recovery approaches adapted from the Minnesota Model. White's Recovery Management model adapted from the Minnesota Model includes recovery coaching (peer recovery support specialist) and was developed by William White in 2006.

Schuyler developed a professional model of life coaching for addiction recovery by blending the Minnesota Model and Harm Reduction model with the core competencies of the International Coach Federation (ICF).

I would like to focus on professional recovery coaching. There is also peer recovery coaching. Professional-recovery coaches receive professional training that involves certain competencies such as ethics, action planning, active listening, powerful questioning, legal responsibilities, and referral through disengagement, interactive and written testing, and much more. Professional-recovery coaching is a client and results driven service that is a form of strengths-based support for those persons with addictions, or in recovery from alcohol or drug dependence, process addictions, codependency, and other addictive behaviors.

Professional-recovery coaches do not diagnose, provide primary treatment, and don't subscribe to any particular modality of treatment. The coaches don't deal with any mental-health issues. They don't do therapy or any form of counseling. Professional-recovery coaching is action oriented, emphasizing improving present life and achieving future goals.

Bob Timmons, a California-based addiction specialist, is recognized as introducing recovery coaching into the mainstream in 1986. He assisted a famous rock band to find sobriety from heroin addiction.

Today there are coaching specializations within the niche of professional coaching. For example, within the field of professional recovery coaching, there is family recovery coaching, gambling addiction coaching, sex addiction coaching, and others. Professional recovery and family recovery coaches are an invaluable tool to help families and their addicted loved ones through the healing process. Coaches can help you and your loved ones find the answers and the solutions that you may not be able to find on your own.

These are highly trained professionals with skill sets, tools, and the experience to help save lives.

Addiction: A mental obsession, disease of the mind that allows the addicted person to continue the behavior despite the negative consequences coupled with the disease of the body, or phenomenon of craving once they use, they can't stop. Can't use, can't quit, a hopeless condition that causes a malady of the spirit. Process addictions are behaviors vs. drugs or alcohol.

Therapist/Counselor: A licensed and trained practitioner who does therapy. Psychotherapy is a general term referring to therapeutic interaction or treatment contracted between a trained professional and a client, patient, family, couple, or group. The problems addressed are psychological in nature and of no specific kind or degree, but rather depend on the specialty of the practitioner.

Psychotherapists utilize a range of techniques, skills, and activities based on experiential relationship building, dialogue, communication and behavior change that are designed to improve the mental health of a client or patient, or to improve group relationships (such as in a family).

Sponsor: The Twelve Steps and the Twelve Traditions to their respective primary purposes. Sponsors are unpaid, untrained individuals that have completed the program and are sober for a length of time, hopefully at least one year. A sponsor is a guide through the steps for a person new to recovery who usually belongs to a twelve-step fellowship such as AA or NA.

Life Coach: Life coaching is a client and results driven practice that helps people identify and achieve personal goals. Life coaches assist clients by using a variety of tools, core competencies, skills, and techniques. Life coaching draws inspiration from disciplines such as sociology, psychology, and positive adult development.

However, coaches are not necessarily therapists or consultants; psychological intervention and business analysis may be outside the scope of some coaches' work.

On August 14, 2012, the word Life Coach was listed for the first time in the mainstream Merriam-Webster's Collegiate Dictionary.

Types and Niches:
1. Business Coaching
2. Personal Coaching
3. Christian Coaching
4. Executive Coaching
5. Career Coaching
6. Financial Coaching
7. Health and Wellness Coaching
8. Sports coaching
9. Dating and Relationship Coaching
10. Recovery coaching

Sober Companion: A sober companion works "full-time" with the client: full work days, nights, weekends or extended periods where the coach is by the client's side twenty-four hours a day. This is usually for periods of one month or more. Some recovery coach roles have evolved from a travel or sober escort to a Long Term Recovery Coach or Sober Companion. Options begin with treatment discharge, the client's first day or weekend home and may develop into a coaching relationship that continues for several weeks, months or longer.

Recovery support specialist (RSS): Many states are now certifying RSS positions. A recovery support specialist (RSS) or a peer recovery support specialist (PRSS) is a non-clinical person who meets with clients in a community-based recovery center or goes off sight to visit a client. The recovery support specialist ensures there is a contract for engagement, called a personal recovery plan. A key component of the Recovery Management model that all RSS follow is this personal recovery plan.

Peer Recovery support specialists (PRSS) are sometimes called "recovery coaches" but that term has been dropped by William L. White in favor of "recovery support specialist" to avoid confusion with the professional life recovery coach. Other terms used to describe peer recovery support specialist is a peer mentor.

Family Recovery Coach: The family plays such an important role for a person in recovery, yet is so often neglected by traditional models of recovery. Specially trained Family Recovery Coaches strive to create a calm, objective, non-judgmental environment for the family of a recovering substance abuser. These coaches are knowledgeable in specific models that aid the family coping with the changes that they have gone through living with an active substance abuser or living with a recovering substance abuser. FRC will use skill sets, tools, and core competencies to help families of substance abusers reach their goals.

Clinical: A licensed facility with personnel who are trained to practice within a certain scope of medicine within the healthcare system. Medicine is in general conducted within health care systems. In modern clinical practice, doctors assess patients in order to diagnose, treat, and prevent disease using clinical judgment.

Case Management: Referral to disengagement is a collaborative process of assessment, planning, facilitation, advocacy, and care coordination of services and supports. The goal is to meet the substance abuser's or individual's, and family's needs through guidance, support, and linkage to resources.

Engagement: Is the start of any form of relationship between the substance abuser and the professionals, support systems, and helps to change and become sober.

Disengagement: To separate from someone or something, to stop being involved with a person or group: to stop taking part in something.

Assessment: May refer to:
- Educational assessment: documenting the person's knowledge, skills, attitudes, and beliefs
- Health assessment: the specific needs of the client and how those needs will be addressed by the healthcare system.
- Nursing assessment: a patient's physiological, psychological, sociological, and spiritual status
- Psychiatric assessment: a person within a psychiatric or mental health service for the purpose of making a diagnosis.
- A mental health assessment: a person's mental health by a mental health professional such as a psychologist

Service Coordination: Is an advocacy agency supporting adults and children with developmental disabilities to get the services that allow them to fulfill their goals in life.

Referral/Placement: Is a method of promoting products or services to new customers through referrals, usually word of mouth. Such referrals often happen spontaneously, but businesses can influence this through appropriate strategies.

Professional Responsibility: Is the area of legal practice that encompasses the duties of attorneys to act in a professional manner, obey the law, avoid conflicts of interest, and put the interests of clients ahead of their own interests. For other professionals, there is a code of ethics and responsibility.

The Baker Act: The Florida Mental Health Act of 1971 (Florida Statute 394.451-394.47891[1] (2009 rev.)), commonly known as the "Baker Act," allows the involuntary institutionalization and examination of an individual. The Baker Act allows for involuntary examination (what some call emergency or involuntary commitment). It can be initiated by judges, law enforcement officials, physicians, or mental health professionals. There must be evidence that the person: possibly has a mental illness (as defined in the Baker Act).

Is a harm to self, harm to others, or self-neglectful (as defined in the Baker Act)? Examinations may last up to seventy-two hours after a person is deemed medically stable and occur in over a hundred Florida Department of Children and Families-designated receiving facilities statewide. There are many possible outcomes following examination of the patient. This includes the release of the individual to the community (or other community placement), a petition for involuntary inpatient placement (what some call civil commitment), involuntary outpatient placement (what some call outpatient commitment or assisted treatment orders), or voluntary treatment (if the person is competent to consent to voluntary treatment and consents to voluntary treatment). The involuntary outpatient placement language in the Baker Act took effect as part of the Baker Act reform in 2005. The act was named for a Florida state representative from Miami, Maxine Baker, who had a strong interest in mental health issues, served as chair of a House Committee on Mental Health, and was the sponsor of the bill.

The Stark law: Is a limitation on certain physician referrals. It prohibits physician referrals of designated health services ("DHS") for Medicare and Medicaid patients if the physician (or an immediate family member) has a financial relationship with that entity. 42 U.S.C. 1395nn. A financial relationship includes ownership, investment interest, and compensation arrangements. 42 U.S.C. 1395nn(h). The term "referral" is defined more broadly than merely recommending a vendor of DHS to a patient. Instead, the term "referral" means, for Medicare Part B services, "the request by a physician for the item or service" and, for all other services, "the request or establishment of a plan of care by a physician which includes the provision of the designated health service."

DHS includes clinical laboratory services as well as the following: physical therapy services; occupational therapy services; radiology, including magnetic resonance imaging, computerized axial tomography scans, and ultrasound services; radiation therapy services and supplies; durable medical equipment and supplies; nutrients, equipment, and supplies; prosthetics, orthotics, and prosthetic devices; home health services and supplies; outpatient prescription drugs; and inpatient and outpatient hospital services.

The Stark Law contains several exceptions. They include physician services, in-office ancillary services, ownership in publicly traded securities and mutual funds, rental of office space and equipment, bona fide employment relationship, etc.

The law is named for United States Congressman Pete Stark (D-CA) who sponsored the initial bill.

Advocacy: In a legal/law context: An 'advocate' is the title of a specific person who is authorized/appointed (in some way) to speak on behalf of a person in a legal process. See advocate.

Transitional care: Refers to the coordination and continuity of health care during a movement from one healthcare setting to either another or to home, called care transition, between health care practitioners and settings as their condition and care needs change during a chronic or acute illness.

Intervention Specialist: The intervention process is a two-day event starting with only the family first and not the addict or alcoholic. Day one is the pre-intervention where the drug & alcohol intervention specialist spends as much time as necessary with family members, preparing for the actual intervention day and for what happens after it is over. The interventionist has the family and friends write "love letters" to the substance abuser explaining how their addiction is impacting the family.

Everything is done in a spirit of love without enabling. Having a drug & alcohol interventionist is important because they are not emotionally attached to the situation, and it is much easier for us to see the forest for the trees. The interventionist is a professional, has specialized training, understanding, tools, and skills that the family does not have. There is usually anger, resentment, and tension at the intervention so having the drug & alcohol interventionist present makes things run much smoother and opens the door for long-term sobriety for their loved one. Interventions have an amazing way of making their loved one own their addiction and become accountable for themselves, something that has been lacking for a long time. There are several different intervention models that interventionists use depending on the client and the situation.

An intervention: is an orchestrated attempt by one or many people – usually family and friends – to get someone to seek professional help with an addiction or some traumatic event or crisis, or other serious problem. The term intervention is most often used when the traumatic event involves addiction to drugs or other items. Intervention can also refer to the act of using a similar technique within a therapy session. An intervention can be done by a professional interventionist or by friends and family.

Interventions have been used to address serious personal problems, including, but not limited to, alcoholism, compulsive gambling, drug abuse, compulsive eating and other eating disorders, self-harm and being the victim of abuse. There are several different types of interventions, the Johnson model is the one most often used.

Alcohol detoxification: Caution, detoxification from alcoholism can be very dangerous, always consult a medical professional. Detoxification is a process by which a heavy drinker's system is brought back to normal after being used to having alcohol in the body on a continual basis. Serious alcohol addiction results in a decrease in production of GABA, a reuptake inhibitor because alcohol acts to replace it.

Precipitous withdrawal from long-term alcohol addiction without medical management can cause severe health problems and can be fatal. Alcohol detox is not a treatment for alcoholism. After detoxification, other treatments must be undergone to deal with the underlying addiction that caused the alcohol use.

Drug detoxification: Caution, detoxification from drug addiction can be very dangerous, always consult a medical professional. Detoxification is used to reduce or relieve withdrawal symptoms while helping the addicted individual adjust to living without drug use; drug detoxification is not meant to treat addiction but rather an early step in long-term treatment. Detoxification may be achieved drug-free or may use medications, such as Suboxone or Subutex for opiate dependence, as an aspect of treatment. Often drug detoxification and treatment will occur in a community program that lasts several months and takes place in a residential rather than medical center.

Drug detoxification varies depending on the location of treatment, but most detox centers provide treatment to avoid the symptoms of physical withdrawal to alcohol & other drugs. Most also incorporate counseling and therapy during detox to help with the consequences of withdrawal. Post-acute withdrawal symptoms can last for many months after a substance abuser stops using.

Residential Treatment: A residential treatment center (RTC), sometimes called a rehab, is a live-in health care facility providing a recovery program for substance abuse, mental illness, or other behavioral problems. These are structured, positive environments with strict rules.

Recovery: Recovery is a daily reprieve contingent upon the maintenance of one's spiritual condition. A balance and wholeness of body, mind, and spirit. A recovery approach to mental disorder or substance dependence (and from being labeled in those terms) emphasizes and supports a person's potential for recovery.

Recovery is seen in this approach as a personal journey rather than a set outcome, and one that may involve developing hope, a secure base and sense of self, supportive relationships, empowerment, social inclusion, coping skills, and meaning. Other names for the concept are recovery model or recovery-oriented practice.

Originating from the Twelve-Step Program of Alcoholics Anonymous and the civil rights movement, the use of the concept in mental health emerged as deinstitutionalization resulted in more individuals living in the community. It gained impetus as a social movement due to a perceived failure by services or wider society to adequately support social inclusion, and by studies demonstrating that many people do recover. A recovery approach has now been explicitly adopted as the guiding principle of the mental health or substance dependency policies of a number of countries and states. There are many different opinions on what recovery is and should be from the recovery community, the medical community, and other organizations.

(Information gathered from Wikipedia.)

Chapter Sixteen
My Heroes

We grew up with heroes; from books, to celebrities, to green bulky entities that would save us. But I'm seeing that while they are sometimes good role models, my heroes are closer to home.

> *"So much is asked of parents, and so little is given."* –Virginia Satir

My parents were high-school sweethearts; they were married young and spent their entire adult lives together. Their love never ended. My parents were there for me my whole life and no matter what I needed, they were there for me. I was very blessed as a younger man to have two loving and understanding parents who were so committed.

My mom passed on five years ago in March, leaving my father to live alone for the first time in over six decades. Dad has had several surgeries since mom passed, and his health has been declining. He turned eighty-six years old in January; he walks with a walker and often uses a wheelchair. We just found out that his cancer has come back this week; he just started radiation treatments.

My siblings live quite far away, too far to visit my dad very often, so he spends a good amount of time alone. He does have home-health care come in to help him for a few hours every day. I live in the same house; however, I have a separate apartment on the opposite side of the house. I am also in a wheelchair and have been for almost five years now. Even though my dad can't walk very well, up until recently, he was able to walk better than I could. It has been a cruel fate that we haven't been able to see each other much and both spent too much time alone.

I made it my priority to spend time with him no matter how much pain I am in. I have visited him daily for the past few months; what a tremendous blessing it has been for us both! Just to see my dad smile makes any pain well worth it for me. I can see that he looks forward to my afternoon and evening visits, and they do lift his spirits.

In addiction all substance abusers do, is take and take from their parents; they cause all kinds of stress as parents wait for the phone to ring; that call that their addicted child is dead, in jail, or in the hospital; it's a horrible way to live.

In recovery, trust is built between the son or daughter and the parents again over time.

One of the greatest gifts of my life in recovery has been being a good son again. Being there for my mom when she passed, and I was able to spend all those good years with her previously.

Now being there for dad and spending time with him, supporting him in his time of need. He's having his sixth cancer surgery in a few days, and I know it will be high risk at dad's age. I have faith that everything will turn out just fine; dad is a tough United-States Air Force Vet.

Most of the time, he'll just sit quietly in his recliner and watch the television with me. We talk a little bit, and he'll nod off. I'll stay a few hours after he falls asleep and an aid will come and help him up to bed.

He'll usually ask, "Are you coming over tomorrow?" You know the answer is yes! I couldn't stand to think of dad sitting there alone all afternoon and evening. I love him too much for that!

I know our time together on this earth is running out. We both are Christians, so that's all right with us because of our beliefs. It's the little things that bless me most these days and that I appreciate the most:

- Good talks with family or friends
- Spending time with my dogs
- Writing, writing, writing
- The star-lit Pennsylvania sky
- Good soup
- A good poem
- My dogs, who are usually sleeping under the blanket on my legs
- Fall days
- Learning
- Teaching
- The quiet
- Music
- A nice hot shower
- Life itself

There used to be so many things that I took for granted. I thought that the world owed me a living that I deserved to be entertained all the time. I believed that I needed to live life in the fast lane, faster, faster, faster, every day! I was missing the best things in life, the simple joys. If I could teach young people anything today, I would say,

- Slow down
- Don't do drugs
- Listen to older people, they have lived a long time and have wisdom
- Life is short, don't take yourself so seriously
- Take more risks
- Take care of your body, it's the only one you get
- Be kind to senior citizens; you will be old someday too
- We are our brother's and sister's keepers
- Love is more powerful than anything else
- Don't forget to breathe
- Don't forget to look
- Don't let anyone take your voice
- Don't let anyone hurt you or the people you love
- Hard work pays off; smart work pays off

- **Be kind to yourself and others**
- **Always be a student of life**

I know that not all people are as blessed as I have been to have such great parents. I learned some great lessons from my parents; although, they made their share of mistakes over the years, they did the best that they could. I couldn't be prouder of who my mother was and who my father is; they truly are my heroes, the ones who showed me how to live and be a kind and caring person. I will forever be in their debt. It's the little things in life that are the greatest blessings! My mother and father gave all that they had to help the sons and daughters of strangers who suffered from addiction problems. I'm so proud to be their son. This book is dedicated to my amazing parents.

Rev. Dr. Kev.'s Publication Credits

Phase II Christian Coaching, LLC Amazon.com *If You Want What We Have; A Journey Through the Twelve Steps of Recovery Workbook and Manual* 2015 Made the Amazon.com Top 100 Best Seller list.
Phase II Christian Coaching, LLC Amazon.com In The Sunlight of the Spirit Workbook and Manual
Tumbleweeds; Feather Books Poetry Series A Book of Poetry Written by Rev. Kevin T. Coughlin Feather Books England May 2002 (In Memory of DeWitt)
The Aurorean, Encircle Publications 1998 Poetry and Essays
Joel's House Publications 1998-2005 Poetry and Essays
Our Journey 1998-2005 Poetry
The Poetry Explosion, The Pen 1999-2003 Poetry
Apostrophe 1998 Poetry
Nuthouse Twin Rivers Press 1998 Poetry
The National Library of Poetry 1998
Lines N' Rhymes 1998 Poetry
The Poetry Church Feather Books
England. Anthology John Hunt Publications 1999 Poetry
A Tapestry in Time. 1999 Poetry Book 18 Poems
Connecticut Department of Mental Health and Addiction Services
The Webster Times 1999 Poetry
The Angel News 1999 Poetry
The Skater won The Editor's Choice Award September 1999 (Our Journey)
The Blind Man's Rainbow 1999 Poetry
Arnazella 2001 Poetry
Feather Books, The Poetry Church 1998-2002
The American Dissident 2002 Poetry
The Good Shepherd Poetry 2002
Ya ' Sou Magazine Essays and Poetry
Colt. Winner Editor's Choice Award Contest Literally Horses 2002
Goodbye My Friend Read on the Radio Rhyme and Reason UBC Europe & the UK September 2001 Read on the Radio in

Europe and the UK as a Tribute to those lost on September 11th bombings. My poem was read over the radio for many days.
Tumbleweed Read on BBC Radio in England 2001
Published by Feather Books
Notified by John Waddington Feather that Tumbleweed had been read on BBC Radio in England on Several Occasions.
Stanwich Congregational Flyer Poetry
University of Scranton Panuska College of Professionals Essay 2002
Scranton University 2002 Poetry
The River Reporter Newspaper 2002 Poetry
Unity Community News 2002 Poetry
The Poetry Corner Angelfire.com Poetry
The Poet's Market 2002 Poetry
The Poetry Church England 2003 Poetry
Cover of Wayne Independent News 2003 Poetry
Nomad's Choir 2003 Poetry
Written a series of 9 course manuals for a coaching recovery curriculum. 2014-2015
www.addictedminds.org 2015-2016 Articles Matthew Steiner
www.soberservices.com 2015 Articles
http://fromaddict2advocate.blogspot 2016 Articles Marilyn Davis
LinkedIn 2014-2016 Articles
Two Drops of Ink S.W. Biddulph 2015 Poetry
The Addict's Mom 2016 Articles Blog
Ghostwriter Articles/ Content 2014-2016
CBS News Channel 10
NBC KHQ Q6 News
NBC Eyewitness News 8 KLKN TV
Fox 14 News at 9
Wayne Independent Newspaper Honesdale, PA
News Eagle, Hawley, PA
Reading Eagle, Reading, PA Berks & Beyond
Blog Talk Radio The Broken Brain
www.eatingdisorderhope.com

About The Author

Rev. Dr., Kevin T. Coughlin Ph.D., is a Master Coach, trainer, writer, poet, speaker, author, a Diplomate Christian counselor, and therapist, he is Board Certified in Family, Developmental, Alcoholism, Substance Abuse, and Grief Counseling, the Reverend is a NCIP interventionist, a Domestic Violence Advocate, Associate Professor for DCU, a Provincial Superintendent (to be consecrated a Bishop in 2016) and so much more; he is an expert in the field of Addiction and Recovery. He was a Founder and Board Member of a Residential Recovery Facility New Beginning Ministry, Inc. and is President and CEO of Phase IIC Coaching, LLC., The Program Director for The Addictions Academy, and the Editor in Chief for Addicted Minds & Associates. The Reverend has over forty-seven years of experience with the AA program. He has been working in the addiction recovery field for almost two decades, has helped thousands of individuals and their families overcome all types of addictions, substance abuse, alcoholism, process addiction, shame and guilt, relationship and communication problems, anger management, inner healing, self-image, interventions and much more. He is a published author and has published thousands of poems and articles published throughout the United States and other Nations, he has been interviewed on numerous radio talk shows and published in magazines, newspapers, books, and online publications. Rev. Kev is a former State, National & World-Champion Powerlifter, and still holds several records. He loves to write, read, teach, listen to music, and spend time with people and dogs. His parents are his heroes.

Thank you for reading my work! If you enjoyed my book, would you consider reviewing it on Amazon.com? I would appreciate your help in getting the word out on how helpful this book is in both understanding the disease of addiction, the solution to addiction, and the program of action to overcome the disease. Thank you so much!

Best of Life!

http://www.amazon.com/Rev.-Kevin-T-Coughlin/e/B01AF6AAAI/ref=ntt_dp_epwbk_0
Rev. Dr. Kev.

Rev. Dr. Kev's Social Media Accounts

Facebook
1. Kevin Coughlin: https://www.facebook.com/profile.php?id=100008449955607
2. My Group, Resources for those suffering from addiction and their families: https://www.facebook.com/groups/resourcesforthosesufferingfromaddiction/
3. RevKev The Addiction Expert: https://www.facebook.com/RevKev/?fref=ts

Linkedin
1. Rev. Dr. Kevin T. Coughlin PhD
   https://www.linkedin.com/in/revkevnetwork

Google+
1. Kevin Coughlin
   https://plus.google.com/112400908736308001821/posts
   My Group: The Recovery Community Family and Friends:
   https://plus.google.com/communities/113521225141112811207

Pinterest
1. Kevin Coughlin: https://www.pinterest.com/ktc1961/
2. My Group Board: Recovery We Can
   https://www.pinterest.com/ktc1961/recovery-we-can/

Tumblr
1. https://www.tumblr.com/blog/revkevsrecoveryworld

Instagram
theaddiction.expert

My Websites:
1. www.revkevsrecoveryworld.com
2. theaddiction.expert
3. theaddiction.guru

Rev. Kev's Goodreads Link:

https://www.goodreads.com/author/show/14874631.Kevin_Coughlin

About.me Link: https://about.me/ktc1961/

http://ilikeebooks.com/if-you-want-what-we-have/
http://awesomegang.com
www.amazon.com/Rev.-Kevin-TCoughlin/e/B01AF6AAAI/ref=ntt_dp_epwbk_0
http://mybookplace.net/in-the-sunlight-of-the-spirit-a-spirituality-training-manual-and-workbook-by-kevin-coughlin/

www.ingramcontent.com/pod-product-compliance
Lightning Source LLC
Chambersburg PA
CBHW070556170426
43201CB00012B/1856